This w
she could have
Aneel Rawal was quite int
list. In fact, he wouldn't have even
the list.

Yet here he was, the cheater. Why was he in crisp chef's whites? And how did he know her boss, Deepak?

Whatever the reason, it was not good.

"Deepak," she said, fixing her death glare on Aneel. "What is he doing here?"

"Oh." Deepak cleared his throat. "You two...ah...know each other?"

"Unfortunately," Karina answered, still trying to melt Aneel as he stood before her. Aneel, for his part, simply stared at her, his jaw clenched, dark eyes clouding over with anger or surprise. He looked exactly as he had seven years ago.

Well, maybe not exactly. He was broader, like his whites finally fit him properly. All of him seemed more filled out, in fact. The dark eyes were the same, the same glint of amusement—or was it irritation?—that had been there all those years ago. His lips were pressed together in annoyance, that beautiful jaw set. Humph. So maybe time had been more than kind to him. It did not matter. Not one bit.

"So...uh...well, there seems to be some tension between you." Deepak's grin widened. "That's even better."

Dear Reader,

Welcome once again to Harlequin Special Edition! I'm really excited to share this story with you. Karina is a single mom (sister to Rani, whom you met in *Their Accidental Honeymoon*), and she's doing the best she can. She moved back in to her childhood home when her son's father took off to go find himself. She's now a chef and mom to five-year-old Veer, and she's up for a promotion!

Who knew she'd have to compete for it on a reality TV cooking show against her former nemesis, Aneel Rawal.

Aneel has raised his sister and struggled to make ends meet, but now he's in the running to become head chef. This will make a big difference in his life. He just didn't know he'd be pitted against Karina Mistry for the spot.

Things heat up between this grumpy-sunshine duo, in the kitchen and out. But when Veer's biological father shows up and wants to be part of Karina's and Veer's lives again, what will she choose?

I hope you enjoy this single mom's opposites-attract journey!

As always, I love hearing from you!

Please come say hi!

Best,

Mona Shroff

Instagram: @MonaShroffAuthor

Website: MonaDShroff.com

IF YOU CAN'T STAND THE HEAT...

MONA SHROFF

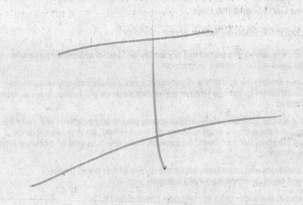

Harlequin

SPECIAL EDITION

Harlequin®
SPECIAL
EDITION™

Recycling programs for this product may not exist in your area.

ISBN-13: 978-1-335-40235-6

If You Can't Stand the Heat...

Copyright © 2025 by Mona Shroff

Harlequin Enterprises ULC
22 Adelaide St. West, 41st Floor
Toronto, Ontario M5H 4E3, Canada
www.Harlequin.com

Printed in Lithuania

MIX
Paper | Supporting responsible forestry
FSC® C021394

Mona Shroff has always been obsessed with everything romantic, so it's fitting that she writes romantic stories by night, even though she's an optometrist by day. If she's not writing, she's likely to be making melt-in-your-mouth chocolate truffles, reading, or raising a glass of her favorite gin and tonic with friends and family. She's blessed with an amazing daughter and a loving son, who have both left the nest! Mona lives in Maryland with her romance-loving husband and their rescue dog, Nala.

Books by Mona Shroff

Harlequin Special Edition

Road Trip Rivalry

Once Upon a Wedding

The Five-Day Reunion
Matched by Masala
No Rings Attached
The Business Between Them
Their Accidental Honeymoon
If You Can't Stand the Heat...

Visit the Author Profile page
at Harlequin.com for more titles.

Nilay, Ami and Mohit—you waited your turn, and I know you learned how to cook making those Christmas dinners

Chapter One

"Mommy."

"Hmm." Karina Mistry tucked her braid up and into a low bun as she caught her young son's image in the mirror. He held out a small piece of paper toward her.

"I made you something." Dark eyes gleamed at her from under equally dark and unruly hair. His Captain America T-shirt was stained with turmeric and something brown she hoped was chocolate.

She turned to look at him, her smile getting broader. Veer was only four, but already the baby fat was leaving his cheeks. He'd grown a couple inches these past few months so his pants were a bit short. Not to mention, sometimes he sounded like a wizened old man. The eyes and hair, he got from his father, the light brown skin he got from her.

She pushed aside thoughts of her ex-husband. No matter now. Veer had her dad, as well as her new brother-in-law, Param, as two very positive male figures in his life. That would have to be enough.

Karina took the offered paper. Veer had written *good luck* and drawn what must be her in her chef's whites, holding an award. Her heart swelled over, misting her eyes. "Thank you." She beamed at him.

"That's the award you get when you are 'secutive chef," Veer told her. "Param Mama told me."

"Thank you for the card, I love it." She hugged her baby-who-wasn't-a-baby-anymore. She inhaled deeply as he squeezed her back. These hugs would never get old. *Please don't let him ever stop hugging like this.* He smelled of baby powder and lotion and...and maple syrup.

"Did you get syrup all over you again?"

Veer pulled back and looked her in the eye. "Maybe."

She sighed and picked him up. Not as easy as it used to be. She set him on the counter in their small bathroom and ran warm water over a washcloth. Veer sat still while she hunted for the random spots of maple syrup, which she found on his elbows and neck. She wiped him as clean as she could. He really needed a bath, but then she'd be really late. Lucky she hadn't put on her chef's whites yet. She would be wearing her "good" ones today. The ones she saved for special occasions. "How'd you get it on your neck?"

Her child shrugged. "If my dad was here, he could give me a bath me so you could go to work," Veer said.

Karina sighed but did not comment. He had been asking about his dad daily since he'd learned about different types of families in school. "You have a dad," he had said. "Where's mine?"

Karina sighed. How was she supposed to tell a four-year-old that his father had bailed before he was born to go find himself. Chirag had simply told her that he needed time and wasn't ready to be a father. He didn't slink off in the middle of the night, but he really hadn't given much explanation, either. He had been gone a couple weeks when her father convinced her to move back to her childhood home. It was tight, with her two sisters still there, but they had managed. Her youngest sister, Rani, had only recently moved out after getting married.

Param called from downstairs. "Sorry, I got held up at after-school play practice." He was at the bedroom door in no time.

"Param Mama!" Veer screeched and jumped off the bed to embrace his uncle. Param knelt down and squeezed him back.

Karina's heart warmed. Rani had chosen her husband wisely. Not to mention that her family and Param's family all grew up together. "So, he might be sticky from maple syrup. I tried to get it off, but…" She raised her hands in a gesture of surrender and shook her head. "He may need a bath. Dad has a late meeting. And Sona," she sighed. "Sona is on a shoot, I believe, in Virginia, but should be back later tonight."

This was their regular run-down, passing of the baton, so to speak. Param was great with Veer, and Karina needed her village. Between her father, her two sisters and Param, Veer was well cared for. Being a chef was demanding, but she was good at it, and she loved it. Even if her boss was a bit eccentric at times.

Deepak Shah had hired her to wash dishes at Fusion when she started culinary school. He had moved her up to line cook and by the time she had graduated, she was a sous chef. She was currently the head sous chef. In the years she had known Deepak, he'd been fair, but he had also been demanding, and really never let her forget that he was the boss. Never mind that he was a businessman and not a chef, it was always clear who ran the show. He didn't interfere with the cooking, but he did attempt changes in menu that were not always plausible. But she and the staff always had to try, regardless.

But today, all her hard work was going to pay off. She had worked harder than anyone else in that kitchen. Carlos, the executive chef had given notice a couple weeks ago and his last day had been a week ago. Karina had easily taken over, as she had been closely working with Carlos for years, and this was the payoff. She was sure of it.

Deepak had called this meeting with her two days ago. Today, Deepak was going to name the new executive chef, she was sure of it. She was confident of her abilities. She deserved the promotion. Sure it was more work, but it was also more money. More money meant she could plan for her and Veer's future, contribute more to the household and possibly move into their own place. She wouldn't go far, she loved having her family to lean on. Her dad loved having them here, and she loved being here, but she really wanted to be on her own.

"Okay. I need to go." Karina grabbed her chef's whites and bent to kiss Veer, picking up her to-go mug of coffee. "Thanks so much, Param."

"No problem." He grinned. "I'd say good luck, but this promotion belongs to you already."

"I see why my sister married you." She smiled at him.

Param rolled his eyes, and a slight flush came over his face. "Mommy is being nice to Param Mama," he said to Veer. "She must be very nervous."

Karina shook her head at Param and left. Damn straight this promotion was hers.

Chapter Two

Aneel finished making dinner for his sister and quickly scrubbed the pans. Saira would return late tonight; the last thing she needed after a grueling day at veterinary school was to have to deal with dishes.

His phone buzzed. FaceTime. Saira. He carefully propped his phone beside the sink and tapped it open. "Hi."

"Stop doing the dishes and go to work. Today is the big day. If you're late, they won't be able to celebrate you."

"You don't know I'm getting the promotion."

"Why else would they ask you to the flagship restaurant?"

"Saira, it's hardly a flagship if it's not making money." He rinsed the last dish and set it on the dish mat.

"That's only because you're not the executive chef yet. Just wait until you're running things there. It's going to explode!" Saira was seven years his junior. She currently had her dark, unruly curls in a ponytail. She must be walking toward the clinic; he could see the tall buildings of Baltimore behind her.

Aneel could not help the grin that was coming over his face. His little sister was not so little anymore. "I'm supposed to do the pep talks. I'm the big brother." He chuckled as he washed and dried his hands.

Saira rolled her eyes. "Oh my god, Bhaiya! Just go to work. Grab that promotion."

He pressed his lips together. "Yeah. I'll get right on that."

It wan't that he didn't think he deserved the position, it was simply that he was skeptical that his boss would give it to him. Aneel had worked his way up from washing dishes at Chutney Catering, which was the sister company to Fusion Restaurant. He had done anything and everything that was asked of him. Over the years, he had acquired the skills needed to run the kitchen at either Fusion or Chutney. But currently, Chutney was not promoting, and Fusion was. Aneel knew that Deepak was desperate for a change at Fusion, since the restaurant was not doing well financially. So he wasn't surprised when Deepak had asked him to come to Fusion this morning to discuss the future of the restaurant and Aneel's role in it.

"Mom would be so proud of you," Saira said softly, stopping her movement to look directly at him.

He inhaled deeply. "You, too." Their mother had passed close to ten years ago, but the ache was still there. A single mom, her every action had been for them.

"I gotta go." Saira glanced at something he could not see. "Good luck. And thanks for dinner."

He dismissed her thanks with a wave of his hand. "I'll be late."

"As always." She sighed. "Do you think you might get more regular hours with this promotion? It's hard finding a wife if you're working all the time."

His twenty-seven-year-old sister could give their matchmaking aunties a run for their money. "Bye!" he said loudly, then disconnected the call.

The sudden silence was jarring. His phone buzzed again. Tyler. Aneel smiled. Tyler was his best friend from childhood. More family than anything else. Aneel and Saira had spent more nights than not at Tyler's growing up, especially when their mother had to work late. Aneel was as comfortable in Mrs. Hart's kitchen as he was in his own.

Today Tyler sent him a good luck GIF that included showing him the middle finger. Aneel chuckled and sent him a rude gesture back.

Aneel grabbed his pressed chef's whites and locked the door on his way out. He took the steps to the ground floor of their building. He wasn't fast enough to bypass Tara Auntie and her daughter, Dolly, who was the same age as his sister. Dolly was forever experimenting with her look. Today, her dark hair was slicked straight, her eyes were heavily lined with kohl and she was attired head to toe in black. Aneel narrowed his eyes. Was she wearing leather pants? Tara Auntie was the same as always, in a sparkly cotton salwar kameez, her hair oiled and in a tight braid down her back.

"Aneel!" Auntie grinned at him. "Off in such a hurry?"

Aneel responded with a wave. "Hi, Auntie. How's it going, Dolly?"

Dolly rolled her eyes behind her mother's back as Auntie answered, "Great, great. And how are you, beta?"

"I'm late for work, Auntie."

"Of course. Don't let me stop you."

"Thanks." Aneel started to walk away.

"You know," Auntie continued even as Aneel took a step away, "Dolly is also quite the cook. You two could work wonders in the kitchen together." Auntie smirked, before continuing to simper, "I'm sure she would love to learn how you make your butter chicken."

"Mom. Seriously." Dolly shook her head and didn't even flush. Her mother's matchmaking was constant and unparalleled. "I don't even eat meat. Go to work, Aneel."

Aneel left. The aunties in his building were on a mission to find him a wife. Not that he wasn't interested in being married, but he was busy doing other things right now. He found his car in the apartment garage and left for the restaurant.

He found a spot in the back parking lot of Fusion, which was a rarity, so it boded well for him today. The air was warm for early September, and the rain that had threatened all day, held off, as if nature itself was rooting for him to get the promotion. Aneel gathered his whites from the car and entered the back of the restaurant. He ducked into the locker room, donned his whites and checked his phone. One minute to spare. He smiled to himself.

This was finally going to happen. Everything he'd worked for over the past eight years. Line cook, sous chef, practicing technique at home, working double shifts to pay for Saira's college and save for her vet school. All of it was coming to a head. Once he was appointed executive chef, his pay would significantly increase, there would be benefits, and he'd be able to keep Saira from needing a loan to finish school.

Not to mention, running this kitchen would bring him closer to owning his own place.

Today was the day his life would change. Time to take a giant leap forward.

He exited the locker room into the hallway, his heart light, a smile on his face. His boss, Deepak Shah, had wanted to meet in the bar. Of course he did. Deepak never had meetings in an office.

Aneel turned the corner into the main dining area and walked across to the bar. Deepak was there, hair disheveled as was usual, in a faded long sleeve t-shirt and jeans, speaking to someone in chef's whites. Must be the sous chef.

Aneel walked up and held his hand out to greet Deepak, not yet glancing at the sous chef, so Deepak had his full attention. He caught a pleasant whiff of something familiar, citrusy, but put it out of his mind.

"Deepak. Excited to see you," Aneel said, shaking his boss's hand.

Deepak grinned. "You, too." His boss glanced at the sous chef beside Aneel. "You know Chef Mistry?"

Aneel turned to face the woman, even as the name pounded in his head. He only knew one Chef Mistry.

Sure enough, standing beside him, in crisp chef's whites, her hazel eyes reflecting the surprise and angst that was building inside him, her mouth slightly open, was Chef Karina Mistry. The surprise in her eyes quickly turned to animosity. It had been seven years—and she *remembered him.* His breath caught, and his heart thudded in chest. Which was pretty much his reaction to her every time he'd been in her presence all those years ago.

That reaction was, however, completely unacceptable now. He wasn't quite sure why she was here, but it did not seem like a good sign.

She narrowed her eyes at him and hissed, "You!"

He raised an eyebrow, forcing himself to appear cool and unaffected by her presence, even as his heart continued to thud extra hard and extra loud. As if his heart had known she would be here. "Me."

Chapter Three

This couldn't be happening. Of all the people she could have expected to see today, Aneel Rawal was quite literally last on her list. In fact, he wouldn't have even made the list.

Yet here he was. Forget that he was taller than she remembered. Though she wished she did not. She ran her gaze over him as she hissed. *Why* was he in crisp chef's whites? And how did he know her boss, Deepak?

Whatever the reason. It was not going to be good for her.

"Deepak," she said, fixing her death stare on Aneel. It was the stare she had used when she needed her sisters to listen. These days she used it on Veer, too. She was *not* taking in how much more handsome Aneel was than the last time she'd seen him. How he had seemed to improve with age. Like some fine vintage she'd studied in culinary school. What she wouldn't give for laser beam eyes right now, to be able to fry him to a crisp. She made a mental note to ask Veer which Avenger had that skill. Or was it one of the X-men? "What is *he* doing here? In chef's whites?"

"Oh." Deepak cleared his throat. "You two…ah…know each other?"

"Unfortunately," Karina answered, still trying to melt Aneel as he stood before her. Aneel, for his part, simply stared at her, his jaw clenched, dark eyes clouding over with anger or surprise. It made no difference. He looked exactly as he had seven years ago.

Well, maybe not *exactly*. He was broader, like his whites finally fit him properly. Or too tight, if she was honest. All of him seemed more filled out, in fact. The dark eyes were the same, the same glint of amusement—or was it irritation—that had been there all those years ago. His mouth was pressed together in annoyance, that beautiful jaw set. Hmph. So maybe time had been more than kind to him. It did not matter. Not one bit.

"So…uh…well, there seems to be some tension between you." Deepak's ridiculous grin widened. "That's even better."

Something in his voice made Karina snap her head to him.

She narrowed her eyes as things clicked into place. Of course, if she was no longer head sous chef, Deepak would have to replace her. Jacob was the natural choice to replace her, but maybe Deepak had other plans for Jacob, and therefore needed Aneel to step in as sous chef.

Which meant she had to work with him. She inhaled and straightened to face Deepak. At least she would outrank Aneel. "How is that better?"

"Well." Deepak swallowed and faced them. "I have brought you both here today, because you are both skilled and talented chefs, which means you're both eligible for the the executive chef position."

A pit formed in her stomach. Deepak could not possibly be considering giving the position to *Aneel Rawal*. But then why ask her to be here. No, her gut told her, there was more. And she was not going to like it.

"I have made no secret as to the fact that Fusion is not doing well financially." He paused. "That's not to say that your considerable talents couldn't bring in more customers. Honestly, I was considering hiring you both to fill the position, co-executive chefs, as it were." Deepak paused and grinned as if this idea was fantastic.

Karina simply stared at him, her fists balling at her sides. Beside her, she felt Aneel tense as well. She would not deign to look at him.

"But then," Deepak raised a finger and smirked, "I realized that it wasn't the talent.The food, the ambiance, the service was all fabulous. Maybe people did not eat here because they did not know about it." He clapped his hands together. "Publicity. That's what we need." He nodded at them as if this was all self-explanantory.

Neither she nor Aneel spoke. She held her breath and waited for the bomb to fall.

"We have been offered an opportunity to do a reality show. Here at the restaurant." Deepak raised his hands and beamed as if this was the most wonderful idea ever.

The pit in Karina's stomach churned. She blinked, unable— no, unwilling—to comprehend the words he had just said. Beside her, it seemed Aneel was as taken aback as she was.

"No," Karina finally said, the echo of Aneel's hard "no" next to her.

She didn't even need to look at Aneel. His anger was rippling off of him in his increased breath, and low murmured curse in Gujarati.

When Aneel spoke, it was a low, but firm growl. "I'm not going on TV."

"Neither am I," Karina agreed. "Not only that, I'm not competing for a position that is rightfully mine. I have worked my ass off in this restaurant for the past five years. I have done every job from dishwasher to sous chef to manager when you're not around. That job is mine."

"I am equally qualified." Aneel leaned toward Deepak, his voice gruff. "I have been working for you at Chutney Catering for the past seven years doing everything, including getting clients."

Karina snapped her head to him. "You work at Chutney Catering?"

"For the past seven years," Aneel repeated.

Karina turned to Deepak. "*I* applied to Catering."

"Aneel was already working there. I needed someone here at Fusion. I told you that when I hired you." Deepak's answer was dismissive. He had done what was right for the business. Made sense.

It was true. She'd simply had no idea that Aneel Rawal was the reason she couldn't work on the catering side. She'd applied to Catering because that was what she really liked. Parties and weddings, graduations. Being able to plan a menu for several hundred people was a challenge she excelled in. Fusion was fine, but the pace of the restaurant was overwhelming at times. She learned how to handle the pace and how to effectively run a fast paced kitchen. She had managed, because a job was a job and she'd needed it back then, as much as she wanted it now.

"In any case," Deepak continued, "the reality show is set. You are both my first choices for this. If you refuse to do the reality show, we'll be parting ways. I need to make this restaurant work, or my dad is going to make me go to law school." He shuddered. "It's local TV, WBAL. My cousin, Rakesh, works there. He'll be the producer, and he'll bring a small camera crew. We need the local publicity. We've got to get more customers coming in. This could be our best chance to do that. People love a reality show."

Deepak rested his gaze on her. Karina just stared at him, hoping that somehow his words were not actually true.

He shifted his gaze to Aneel and pressed his lips together. "Look. I get it. It's a lot to throw at you, but it just cleared a couple days ago," Deepak said pleasantly, just a hint of apology in his voice. "The show is four weeks. Every Monday, you will each prepare a meal, on camera, based on a menu that will be chosen for you. Our local judges will judge the meals for taste, presentation and originality. Whoever the winner is, will then be the head chef at Fusion for that week. The cameras will take footage of your leadership, the kitchen, whatever the people want to see. At the end of the four weeks, the viewers and judges will have a final vote, and we'll have a new executive chef." Deepak inhaled deeply. "It's perfect, the viewers get to pick who runs the restaurant, then they come down and sample the food. It's win-win."

Karina stared at him. Deepak had lost his mind completely this time. "What about us? How is it win-win for *us*?"

Deepak looked at her like she was a child. "One of you will be executive chef. The other will be the head sous chef. You'll both have jobs."

"We both have jobs now," Aneel interjected.

"If you do the show." Deepak seemed agitated. "Look. I need two qualified chefs to participate in this show. You two are the best I have. But if you won't do it, I need to find someone who will. This show is happening."

Deepak's phone buzzed. He glanced at it. "It's Rakesh. I have to take this. Look, I can give you to the end of shift tonight to let me know. But that's it." He put his phone to his ear and walked away.

"I always knew he was a bit out there, but this is a new level," Aneel mumbled.

Karina simply glared at Aneel before turning on her heel and walking out. She needed a minute. As much as she hated to admit it, she did agree with Aneel on this—Deepak had hit a new level for sure.

Her phone buzzed with a FaceTime call from Rani. She answered.

"So? Congratulations, right?" Rani asked.

"Not exactly."

"He gave the job to someone else?" Rani's voice went from playful to pissed off in a split second.

Karina sighed. "Not exactly." Where did she even start to explain?

"Karina Ben, you're not making any sense," Rani said.

"Deepak wants us to do a reality show to compete for the executive chef position." Karina couldn't even believe the words she was saying.

"He wants…what?" The confusion on her sister's face mirrored her own unsettled brain.

"A reality show competition."

"With who?"

Karina just shook her head at her sister. She had barely even processed his presence, let alone that she was being asked to enter a competition with him. Again.

"Who, Karina Ben?" Rani's brow furrowed. "Not that it matters. You'll beat whoever—"

"Aneel Rawal." There. She said it.

Rani's jaw dropped. "No. You can't go through that again. With him? That is ridiculous. He cheated last time. You're not going to do it, are you?"

"If I don't, he'll find someone else."

"Then let Deepak worry about finding someone else. There are plenty of restaurants that would love to have you." Rani continued, "What if Aneel cheats again, like he did seven years ago?"

Karina considered it. Rani was not wrong. She had entered that competition seven years ago to get tuition money for culinary school.

The winner of the competition took home the $30,000 prize, presumably for culinary school tuition. The competition had taken place at their local culinary institute, and each person had their own small kitchen station in the large room. But before they had even gotten to that point, there had been smaller competitions. Aneel and Karina were among six finalists to progress to the main kitchens. Every two stations had shared a refrigerator and a freezer.

She was doing really well, but then someone had unplugged her freezer the night before the dessert competition. Her kulfi had been ruined. Aneel denied doing it, but then he had won. His dessert entry that day did not need a freezer or a refrigerator.

There had been an investigation, of course. Aneel had been cleared and the whole thing chalked up to an accident by the cleaning staff.

Karina didn't buy it. The plug was thick, not easily bumped out of place. Someone had pulled it.

But the thought of walking away now out of anger over the past, the idea of Aneel having the executive chef job, made her skin crawl. Why should he get it? He certainly did not deserve it.

"Karina Ben. You cannot compete against him again. He doesn't play fair."

Rani was right. But this job was hers. She wouldn't let Aneel win this time. "I'm doing it," she told her sister. "And I'm going to beat him this time."

Aneel stood frozen to his spot. Deepak had really done it this time. People's jobs weren't a game. This was his livelihood, and he expected him to what? Be in a reality show? He should just hand in his resignation and walk out. There had to be other restaurants hiring.

He let his gaze drift through the window where Karina stood outside. She was on the phone with someone. Likely telling whoever it was that she was up against a cheater again. He could see the accusation all over her face. Even seven years later.

It wasn't worth it. There was no way he was going to compete with Karina Mistry again. Once had been plenty for a lifetime. Saira would be disappointed, but he should be able to find work somewhere else.

He watched her—because let's be real, there was no way to *not* watch Karina Mistry. The woman was a tantalizing force. As he watched, she tapped her phone off with a definitive poke and raised her chin, before turning back to the restaurant and heading for the door. Aneel did not even bother pretending that he wasn't watching her.

Karina reentered and marched right to him.

"I'm doing it," she announced. "I hope you're ready to lose this time."

Aneel had had every intention of backing out. Until he saw the accusation burning like fire in Karina's eyes. It still stung, after all this time, that she thought that poorly of him, that she still accused him of cheating. Before he could think about it too long, the words tumbled from his mouth. "Well then, I guess we have ourselves a rematch."

Chapter Four

It was like no time had passed. Karina Mistry was as infuriating today as she had been seven years ago. The only thing that had changed was that she was more beautiful today than the last time he'd seen her. She had grown into her curves in the most delightful way. Even the drab black slacks and boxy chef's whites could not hide the luscious feminine curves of her body. Those hazel eyes still showed her every emotion, her mouth was perfect even when scowling at him, and he could tell that once she let her hair out of its bondage, it would flow like black silk over her shoulders. She still sipped coffee from a to-go mug.

Had he had a crush on her back then? Of course. All the guys did. Had he hoped to date her after the competition? He had. But that dream had ended when her kulfi melted.

Deepak returned from his phone call and Karina lifted her chin.

"I'm in. For the record, I think this is ridiculous, but I am not about to let him," she flicked her thumb in his direction, "have it. So I'm in."

Deepak grinned at her. "Awesome." He turned to Aneel.

"Yep. You got me too."

Deepak shook their hands. "This is going to be great." Deepak beamed and rubbed his hands together as he led the way to the kitchen, motioning for them to follow.

The three of them walked into the kitchen, Deepak in the lead. The staff was getting ready for dinner service and stopped when Deepak entered.

"Hi, everyone," Deepak said pleasantly. "Just a quick, but very exciting announcement. Chef Mistry and Chef Rawal have agreed to do a reality show here at Fusion." He paused and took in the whole room. "I will need paperwork from all you consenting to this. You have the right to not participate, in which case I can find work for you at Chutney catering, but I really would prefer all hands here."

The staff tensed as a group, looking at one another. A few of them, the sous chef in particular, looked at Karina, a clear question on his face.

"Any questions?"

A general shaking of heads. "Great. Stop by the office after your shift and get your paperwork. We start in a week." Deepak turned to him and Karina. "I have to run. Get service started."

A general murmuring spread across the staff. They eyed Aneel with suspicion. Of course their loyalty was to Karina. Aneel sighed. This was going to be harder than he thought.

"Chef Rawal?" One of the staff approached him.

"Yes?"

"Jacob." He extended a hand. "I'm one of the line cooks here. We met a few years ago. I came over to Catering to help out with a few weddings."

Aneel smiled and nodded. He did remember. Jacob was a hard worker. And talented. He shook Jacob's hand. "Of course. You assembled pani puri shots faster than anyone."

"You know it." Jacob beamed. "It's nice to be acknowl-edged."

Aneel frowned. "Doesn't Chef Mistry acknowledge her help?"

Jacob's eyes widened. "Oh no. That's not what—I mean,

she's busy. There's a lot going on. Deepak can be demanding, you know?"

Yes. Aneel did know. He'd been working with Deepak for close to seven years. But Aneel made sure his staff was appreciated. He glanced at Karina. Clearly that was not a priority for everyone.

He picked up the iPad that had the menu on it. "Okay, everyone gather round. Might as well get started. I'm Chef Rawal. The head chef has already moved on to his next job. I'll be executive chef this week."

"Like hell you will." Karina turned to him. "I made up that menu for this week, and we're sticking with it. The produce and meat have already been purchased, we can't change everything now."

"We most certainly can. The ingredients can be the same, it's all in how it's put together."

"We're not changing it."

"It's my job to change it," Aneel insisted.

"It is not *your job* to do anything around here. Though if you want to help out, I'm sure Jacob could use a night off to spend with his new baby." She smirked at Aneel.

Aneel met her gaze, then nodded at Jacob. "Go enjoy that baby." He grinned. "I got your back."

"Seriously?" Jacob was grinning.

"You're an amazing line cook. I'll do the best that I can to fill your shoes," Aneel said jovially.

Karina stared at him, as if she couldn't believe that someone qualified to be head chef would bother being a line cook.

Aneel looked at her wide-eyed. "Unless you didn't really mean it, Chef."

Karina narrowed her eyes at him. "Of course I meant it." She paused. "Chef." She tossed out the title as if it were an afterthought. Or a taunt.

"Chef Mistry. I can stay," Jacob backtracked.

Karina shook her head and turned to Jacob with a real smile. Aneel knew it was genuine because it lit up her face. "I meant it. You need time with that little one. It's early in the week, and Chef Rawal has volunteered to take your place. Please, run. Before I find something for you to do. Or the good chef changes his mind."

Jacob did not need to be told again. Assured that his job was not on the line, he headed for the locker room.

"Chef Rawal. A word. In my office." Karina left the kitchen and headed down a small hallway. She didn't even look back to see if he followed.

He followed her into a back office, which he suspected had belonged to Carlos until two days ago. Turning around, he steeled himself for the argument he knew was coming his way.

"I do not have to share this kitchen with you until we start this ridiculous game. So my kitchen, my menu, my way." It was apparent that Karina was not about to lose this position— or anything else to him, in addition to what she'd already lost.

Despite this, Aneel challenged her. "Last I checked, you were not named executive chef."

"Neither were you," she shot back. "But as we have no actual head chef, and I am the current sous chef, that makes me the executive chef for now."

Aneel said nothing. He knew she was right.

A knock, and one of the other line cooks, Doneesha, peeked in. "Uh...so the staff needs to get going on dinner service..." She looked at Karina, then Aneel.

"So go ahead as we had planned," Karina said as she stared down Aneel. "Unless Chef Rawal feels this discussion is more important than dinner service."

Aneel shook his head. "Of course not."

Karina grinned in triumph. She just had to get through tonight. Tomorrow was another day, and the competition, well, that wasn't until next week.

She followed Aneel back to the kitchen. She picked up the iPad and gave instructions—bringing the kitchen to life. For her part, she donned a hair net and headed toward the back of the kitchen to start prep. To her annoyance, Aneel followed.

"So you've been here for five years?" he asked.

"Since I graduated." She nodded. "I washed dishes here while I was in school." She pulled out her knife and began cubing the chicken. It was a small kitchen, so regardless of rank, everyone did everything when needed. And they were behind.

He nodded. She did not ask him questions, just continued cutting. She needed to minimize her interaction with him.

"Culinary school taught you that this boring menu would be a hit?"

She looked at him, expecting him to be looking down his nose at her. He was not. In fact, he appeared to be genuinely interested in her opinion.

"Don't you have someone to prep the meat for you?" he continued as he folded his impressive forearms and watched her prep the meat.

"Whenever I can, I like to do it myself," she answered, her voice clipped. "My menu is not boring." She continued to cube the chicken.

"It most certainly is." Again he managed to make his insult not sound insulting—simply informative—like a fact. Even though he was wrong. He pointed to the iPad. "This is traditional South Asian Indian cooking. You can get this at any Indian restaurant in town. Where's the fun? The *fusion*?"

"Our ingredients are superior, and the final product tastes better." Karina spoke with confidence, though by rote. Her mind was on the spices she would need to marinate their chicken.

"That's why you have people lining up?" Aneel smirked. "I would add a fusion aspect. Bring other cultures in. It makes the food unique, fun."

"I didn't ask you."

"You don't have to. Look, here. Instead of just boiled pota-toes in the chaat, make them like French fries. Ooh—or Tater Tots. So many cultures have had an influence on our food, why not the one we live in?" He paused, and a second later his eyes lit up. "Stuff the samosas with a cabbage mixture, adding a Chinese touch, and instead of straight-up tamarind sweet sauce, serve it with hot honey."

Karina just stared at him. "I made that menu. And it stands." The last thing she needed was advice from a cheater.

"Suit yourself, but Fusion is faltering, and I have ideas." Aneel shrugged.

"Great, then you can apply them to the competition and see where that gets you." She brushed past him. "Or you can just cheat."

"I do not cheat."

"You have $30,000 that says you do," Karina snapped.

Aneel narrowed his eyes at her. "You still carry that around?"

"Kind of hard not to. I have loan payments." Karina con-tinued her work.

Aneel just stared at her. "The investigation said it was an accident."

"You were the one who benefitted." She couldn't be both-ered to even look at him. This was old news.

"Still not me. I don't cheat. I had no reason to. Desserts are my strong point. Not yours."

"Unbelievable. Seven years later, and you still have the same story." She shook her head. "At this point, we've fin-ished school and have jobs. Just admit it."

"Why would I admit to something I didn't do? And you're right, it's been seven years, and we both have jobs, why not just let it go?"

Karina had heard of stubborn, but this was unreal. "Fine,

don't 'fess up. I would have had to respect you a little bit if
you did."

"Ever consider that you might not have won even if your
kulfi hadn't melted?" Aneel had the audacity to smirk at her.

"We'll never know now, will we?"

"Make kulfi," Aneel challenged.

She stared at him. "What? Now?" Truth was, she was not
keen on making desserts. It truthfully was not her strong suit.

"We'll ask Deepak to add it into one of the competition
rounds, and we'll see how it turns out," Aneel said.

"So basically you want Deepak to pick an area in which
you excel," she snarked. Typical.

"Fine, you pick an area for a different week."

"Small plates," she blurted out immediately.

"Small plates?"

"Yes." She could not help the smile that fell across her face.
She had created several when she catered her sister Rani's
wedding, and though it was a lot of work, it had been a huge
success. Param still talked about how amazing the pani puri
shooters had been.

There was amusement in his eyes as he watched her. She
stopped smiling.

"Okay," Aneel said. "Small plates one week. Dessert another. We'll let Deepak choose the others."

"Fair enough."

Aneel held out hand to her. "Shake on it?"

She shook his big muscular hand, ignoring the tingle that
shot up her arm at the feel of his callused skin. "We have a
deal."

Chapter Five

Aneel reentered the kitchen behind Karina and took his spot on the line. Apparently, Jacob had been responsible for actually cooking the chicken that Karina had so finely cubed. As such, Aneel got to work gathering the spices needed for this. He placed them in order of use and grabbed a pan.

"Jacob used that pan," a young woman down the line said softly as she nodded at a different pan.

Aneel raised an eyebrow. Unusual choice. "Really?"

She nodded. "The bottom is not as heavy, but the chicken turns out perfect every time."

He glanced at her and nodded. "Thanks." He put away his pan for the one favored by Jacob. Couldn't hurt to give it a try. "I'm Aneel," he said with a smile.

The young woman smiled, a slight flush hitting her cheeks. "We all know," she said. "I'm Marisol."

"Nice to meet you, Marisol," Aneel said as he continued to prep his area. "What do you cook?"

Marisol indicated her station. "I'm on veggies." She nodded to a young man next to her. "This is Scooter. He does fish."

"Nice to meet you, Scooter." Aneel grinned. "Got any advice for me?"

Both Marisol and Scooter froze, their glances drifting behind him.

"Yes." A stern voice came from behind him. Karina. "Less talking and more working."

He turned and was met by those hazel eyes boring into him, her lips in a stern line. He flashed her his best smile. "Just making friends and learning the ropes."

"We are not here to make friends." She glanced behind him. "And you should know how to be a line cook if you're *qualified* to be an executive chef."

"I am more than qualified, Chef." He drew himself up tall. "And I'm always making new friends."

For a split second, he thought he saw an irritated fire in her eyes, but she had it in check before he could really enjoy it.

She grimaced as she glanced over his shoulder at the other two line chefs before stepping back and heading for the prep station.

He turned back to find Marisol and Scooter shaking their heads at him. "She has it out for you." Marisol chuckled.

Aneel shrugged. "It doesn't matter. The food will speak for itself."

Scooter and Marisol shared a grin before shaking their heads and getting to work.

"How is the new job?" Saira asked as Aneel handed her a steaming bowl of khichdi, ghee melted in the middle, just how she liked. It was late, but they had both just come home, him from the restaurant, and Saira from a long day at the veterinary clinic where she was doing her final rotations. He hadn't even seen her last night.

"Well, it's not mine yet."

"What do you mean?"

Aneel scooped himself a bowl of khichdi and sat down across from his sister at the small Formica table in their tiny kitchen. They could have gotten a new one anytime, but this table had been in the kitchen they grew up in. It reminded them of their mother, and they had both silently agreed to keep it.

He had tossed and turned last night thinking about this competition Deepak was forcing them into. He had experience now. He could simply leave and get a job elsewhere. "Deepak is deciding between me and another chef. He has set up a reality show—local only—but still, judges will decide who gets to be head chef." He shook his head. "I should just quit. This is crazy."

Saira raised an eyebrow. "So you have to win to be head chef?"

"Basically, yes, I need to impress the viewers and the judges."

Saira went back to her khichdi. "Of course you'll win. You're the best."

"Thanks, but you're my sister, and therefore, biased."

She scooped khichdi into her mouth and groaned. "Bhaiya. This is the best comfort food on the planet."

He flushed. "Again, you are my sister."

"So, my opinion doesn't count?" She feigned astonishment.

"Not to Deepak or the judges."

"Who is your competition?"

Aneel pressed his lips together at the thought of Karina. Saira laughed.

"What?"

She shook her head, the curls in her ponytail bouncing.

"I just haven't seen you make that face since that competition all those years ago—and you were up against Karina Mistry."

He stared at his sister.

"Oh my god." She dropped her spoon. "It's literally not possible."

"It is," he confirmed.

"You're up against Karina Mistry—again?" The look of

horror on her face mimicked his exact feelings. "Bhaiya. You...you can't..." Her eyes glistened.

"Saira. It's not great, but it's not all that bad either." Aneel reached over and held his sister's hand. "I can handle Karina Mistry."

Saira squeezed his hand, a small smile on her lips. "Of course you can." She nodded and went back to her food. Her phone buzzed next to her. She grabbed for it.

"Hospital?" Aneel asked.

"Hmm?" she asked, distracted as she answered the text. "Um. Yeah. Hospital. I...need to go in."

Aneel snapped his head to her. "You just got home."

"It's fine. I have time to eat," she insisted. Her phone buzzed again, and she furrowed her brow as she read the text.

"Saira. What's going on?"

"Nothing, Bhaiya. Just school." Saira put her phone down. Face down this time.

Chapter Six

Karina came home exhausted and angry. It had already been challenging with some members of the staff since Carlos had left. That was normal, she had been implementing small changes, and staff usually liked keeping status quo. But now that Aneel Rawal was here, making friends with them and chatting and laughing while they cooked, how was she supposed to maintain discipline?

Carlos had run a rather loose kitchen, and Karina believed in discipline. It was how things got done. But Aneel was all about making friends with everyone. Which was ridiculous, because how you could you maintain order if everyone was chatting all the time?

How did a cheater like Aneel get this far in the business? He had of course denied sabotaging her, but it was hard to believe since he took home the prize money. She really could have used that cash. She ended up taking out a loan, so now she was in debt, which was why she was working for Deepak in the first place.

Veer was cuddled up next to Param on the sofa, having been fed and bathed. Param took up the length of the sofa and then some. His feet dangled over the arm even as he slept. Veer was laying on his uncle's broad chest, one of Param's arms securing him. Her son had likely refused to go to his room until Karina came home, and Param had obliged.

"Param," Karina said softly. "Go home."

He started as he woke. "Wha—?"

"Go home to my sister."

"She has the overnight shift at the hospital," he grumbled, his voice heavy with sleep.

"Then go up to her old room," Karina whispered.

Param nodded and carefully sat up, so as not to disturb the sleeping Veer. "He's a great kid, Karina," he told her. "Talks a lot, though."

She grinned, the first real smile of her day, and her heart filled. She needed to sleep as well. Six o'clock would come whether she went to bed now or not. Restaurant hours were long. Late nights were common. Fusion closed the kitchen early compared to other places, so she was usually home by 11:00 p.m. Though once she became executive chef, she was considering keeping the kitchen open longer, to get some of the later crowd.

She picked up her son. He was heavier than she remembered. He was growing so fast. Her heart tugged for a moment. Getting this promotion would mean more time away from him. She was already not home most nights, and the promotion would mean she would miss more things. It also meant a higher income. She could move them into their own place. Save, really save for his education, as well as her retirement.

She really did not have a choice. She was a single mom, she needed this position. Not just for her. But for her son.

All the more reason she needed to do this reality show. Even if it was against Aneel Rawal.

"You're going against Aneel Rawal in a cooking reality show?" Her sister Rani was dressed in scrubs, her wavy hair in a ponytail with flyway pieces framing her round face with bags under her dark eyes. "For the executive chef position?"

She had finished her overnight shift and had stopped by on her way home to see her husband before he left for work.

It was too cute.

Jealousy bloomed in Karina's chest. She wanted that. Though she might as well have wanted a unicorn. She couldn't even maintain friendships. How could she ever manage a relationship? Especially when Veer was not only a part of everything she did but usually the deciding factor.

"I really don't have a choice." She sipped her coffee as she sat at the kitchen island. Rani was at the stove which was in the ample island, boiling water for chai.

"But *Aneel Rawal*! How will you win?"

"Because I am the superior chef," Karina said.

"Duh—but have you forgotten the kulfi?" Rani's eyes widened as she looked up from the pot. Karina was on the stool directly across from her, the kitchen sink behind her. Rani tossed in the loose tea leaves and opened the chai masala container. "No masala?"

Karina shook her head. "Of course I haven't forgotten the kulfi incident." How could she? She had paced and railed to her sisters, but the investigation had cleared anyone from intentional wrongdoing. But Karina just *knew*. Refrigerator plugs didn't come loose.

"Is there more masala?" Rani asked.

"Just Mom's," Karina said and met her sister's eyes. They would never touch that masala. It was all they had left of their mother. That last Ziploc bag of chai masala still in the freezer was a source of comfort for Karina. She knew she always still had a piece of her mother with her.

"Oh." Rani looked a bit lost.

"Just put a stick of cinnamon, a few crushed cardamom pods and a clove or two in the pot. Grate some ginger. It'll be passable." Karina shrugged one shoulder.

Rani did as Karina suggested. "You want some chai?"

Karina shook her head and nearly rolled her eyes at Rani, raising her coffee mug. She didn't drink chai. At least she hadn't in a long while. "I *know* this kitchen," Karina continued. "I've been there since almost the beginning. I can win this competition. Trust me. Everything is on camera. If anything goes wrong, it'll be on tape."

Rani grunted her approval. Param entered the kitchen from the family room, behind Karina, holding a sleepy Veer on his shoulder.

"Hey." Karina set down her mug and walked over and took her son as Param greeted his wife. "How's my little boy?"

"I'm not little," Veer squeaked at her, his voice still groggy with sleep. "I go to school."

Karina chuckled. "Yes. You do." Her son curled up into her, so she grabbed her coffee and left the kitchen to sit on the sofa for a few minutes until Veer had a chance to wake up. They called it his 'defrosting' time.

He curled up next to her with his head on her lap, and she covered him with a cozy blanket. His body might still be small, but he certainly wasn't a baby anymore. He snuggled closer to her, and her heart melted. She tried to do this with him every morning since she wasn't usually home when he got back from school. And he would be asleep when she got home. She rested one arm on him and checked emails with the other, while Veer watched a show on TV.

Email from Deepak. Paperwork and permissions for the network for the reality show. Wow. He was not wasting time. She read through it. Seemed standard. She continued scrolling through messages, and her heart stopped when she saw an email from Chirag. Her ex. She hadn't heard from him since their divorce was finalized almost two years ago.

Her thumb hovered over the email. He hadn't even seen Veer. Hadn't been there when Veer was born, nothing. Sure, they'd had a shotgun wedding in Vegas when she found out she was pregnant. But as her pregnancy progressed, Chirag had panicked and fled. After Veer was born, and he still hadn't come home, Karina had filed for divorce.

After the appropriate waiting period, papers were signed, and she was divorced after hardly being married.

Veer was four years old now. She had plans for him and for her. Why was Chirag emailing now? She tapped open the email, her heart in her stomach.

Hi Karina.

I'm sure you're surprised to hear from me. I understand if you don't respond. I wanted to let you know that I will be in the Baltimore area, and I would like to see you. Just to talk. I have a terrible track record, I know. I have grown these past few years, and I own my mistakes. If you are willing, I would like to meet you for coffee. I would also love to see Veer, but I know that call is not mine to make. Let me know.

Whatever you decide, let me know.

Thank you,

Chirag

Karina was exhausted. How dare he contact her now, after all these years? After never once asking about Veer.

No, she did not want to see him. So what if he had changed? He had left her pregnant and alone and had not once so much as asked to see a picture of his son. She held the phone in both hands, ready to angry-type such a response.

But her thumbs froze over the phone, and in her moment of hesitation, Veer stirred.

She turned off her phone and gave her attention to her son. He did have his father's unruly dark hair, as well as his eyes. Though Karina hardly cared to admit it, there were times that she saw similar facial expressions as well. Her heart swelled with love for Veer so hard, it ached. He deserved better than a father who couldn't be bothered with him.

Her sisters, her father, Param and his family—they had all been there for Veer. For her. She smiled at her son. He had everything he needed, right here.

Chapter Seven

The week went by in a whirlwind. Deepak was looking for a buyer for Chutney Catering, but there was nothing yet. They were still in business, but it was slow, as Deepak turned his focus to Fusion.

Before he knew it, Aneel was sitting in Carlos's old office with Karina next to him while two young men worked on their makeup. Karina did not look like she was any more into having her makeup done than he was. Though he did not bother asking her.

He stole a glance at her. She didn't really need makeup as far as he was concerned. Flawless brown skin, full lips that seemed to be naturally pink and breathtaking hazel eyes. His breath had certainly been robbed the first time he had met her, at that amateur cooking competition.

He had noticed her dishes before he actually met her.

"Aneel Rawal." He held out his hand to her across the aisle between their kitchens.

"Karina Mistry." She smiled and flashed those eyes, and his breath was indeed taken away.

Somehow, he managed to continue conversation with this beauty who was so clearly out of his league. "So, you're K. Mistry. Your dishes looked and smelled amazing. I had to hold myself back from stealing a taste."

"Thanks, A. Rawal. Your desserts looked almost too good

to eat," she responded. "So good thing I couldn't eat them, anyway."

"Thank you. Well. Good luck." He grinned.

"You, too." She smiled again, and Aneel had a hard time tearing his gaze from her.

"Chef Rawal." Deepak was standing in front him.

"Yes." Aneel focused on him, letting the memory fade.

"Chef Mistry is ready to meet the camera crew. Are you?"

"Of course."

Aneel followed Deepak to the kitchen. The camera crew had nearly taken over. If the staff had been cramped before, then they were all on top of each other now. A glance at Karina revealed that she was not any happier about that than he was.

"Tight, isn't it?" he said as he followed Deepak to where Karina was standing.

She shook her head, not even looking at him.

The show's producer, a cousin of Deepak's, walked over to them. "I'm Rakesh, and this kitchen is now my set." Deepak's cousin was a head shorter than Deepak, but with a presence that meant business. He ignored the frowns that Aneel and Karina were making no effort to hide. The kitchen belonged to the chefs, not the TV guy.

Rakesh's voice was powerful as he went over the rules. "Both chefs will make the same dish or dishes, to be judged by Deepak as well as Chef Sonny Pandya and Chef Amar Virani. The desserts will be judged by Chef Divya Shah."

Aneel snapped his head toward the judges. Wow! He'd heard a lot about Amar and Divya, chefs with a hugely successful catering business in their own right. They were recently married and had even catered their own wedding, with their own dessert truck handling the desserts! Amar was tall with a slight beard and Aneel caught a glimpse of Captain America on his t-shirt from his still open chef's whites. Divya was shorter, full of energy which seemed to bubble off her.

Sonny Pandya owned The Masala Hut, one of the best comfort food restaurants around. Aneel had eaten takeout from there many times. Sonny's stuffed paratha were off the hook. Aneel's favorite was the cauliflower and cheese stuffed flatbreads. The spice level was perfection. Right now, Sonny and Amar were laughing as they chatted. If memory served, they went to culinary school together.

Okay, he was impressed. Deepak wasn't messing around. He was getting publicity one way or another.

Aneel glanced at Karina. She had flushed as the judges entered. And now she was fisting her hands. Was she...nervous?

"Okay," Rakesh said. "Today is Monday, the restaurant is closed." He turned to the chefs. "Just go ahead and cook. The menus and ingredients have been provided. The judges will wander and watch. You only have to cook enough for four people."

Aneel nodded and out of the corner of his eye saw Karina do the same beside him.

"This will be aired with a one-week delay. So this week's competition will be viewable by the time you compete next week. We have a sample of viewers at the station watching live. But that's for our feedback, so we can get a sense of what people are particularly interested in. Any questions?"

They shook their heads.

"Get started."

Aneel glanced at his copy of the menu, while Karina did the same. A small smile twisted at her lips. They were doing her type of menu today. Traditional, classic Indian food. Whatever. Aneel could cook anything.

Chicken karahi, any vegetable dish they desired, rice, vegetable biryani, naan. There wasn't detailed instruction, which was a relief, so he could actually express himself a bit in his cooking.

The space was cramped, so they kept bumping into not only

each other but the equipment. More than once, they reached for the same pot or utensil. The ingredients they needed to use were also shared. Quite different than having your own little kitchen station setup as they'd had before.

Aneel added a bit of flair to the biryani, adding diced mango and pomegranate arils to the dish. He glanced over at her a few times during prep and she was laser focused on her quick chopping, grabbing for items without really looking, as if the kitchen were simply an extension of her body. It was beautiful to watch.

For the shaak, he made a simple spinach and paneer dish, and he stuffed the naan with cauliflower and cheese—a la his favorite food at Sonny's restaurant. For dessert, the menu asked for a simple barfi, to which he added guava flavor.

Karina growled at him under her breath as if he was getting in her way on purpose.

"Grumpy much?" he mumbled in return.

"I can hear you."

"Might as well make the best of the situation. We're both stuck here."

"Whatever you say, Sunshine," she said, her tone mocking. But he caught the hint of a smile on her face.

As they prepped, Rakesh was also the moderator of the show, so he pointed out different techniques or ingredients that they were using from off camera.

Amar Virani asked questions and noted their different approaches to the menu. Sonny Pandya came around while they cooked, more interested in their interactions with the staff.

"What do you think, Scooter? You like being on TV?" Aneel asked with a small chuckle. He put his hand out. "Pass me that pan, please? And let's dice those mango pieces evenly."

Scooter smiled and passed the pan. "Sure thing, Chef. Not sure I like being on TV though."

"Marisol. I need you to be more precise in the chopping. We

need a finer chop, or this dish is uncomfortable in the mouth." Karina did not look up from where she sauteed vegetables, as she spoke to Marisol.

"Yes, Chef," Marisol answered.

Karina gave no indication that she had heard the response. She simply kept cooking.

Divya Shah waited to take her tour until they were cutting up the fudge-like milk sweet dessert, barfi, into squares, asking about the flavoring.

"I did the standard cardamom and saffron flavoring," Karina said to Divya. "The saffron I used is a very hard to acquire brand, but its flavor balance is perfect."

"And you, Chef Rawal? How did you flavor your barfi?"

"I tried something new and added guava as opposed to the traditional flavoring. Quality saffron will pull the price point up, but not really give the bang that is desired."

He felt Karina's eyes boring through his back. Whatever. "Quality saffron adds a sophisticated aroma, flavor and color that is authentic," she threw at him.

"That may be true, but as head chef, one has to be aware of the cost and benefits to the ingredients that are used." His response was bland, as if he couldn't be bothered. Which was true. He was in the zone. He added tweaks where necessary, adding a modern touch, keeping things fresh. Everything came out beautifully. No chance he didn't win today.

Time was called, and he and Karina plated everything and presented to the judges. The judges tasted it all, commenting softly to each other.

When they seemed to have reached a decision, Rakesh handed over a microphone. Amar Virani stood. "You're both obviously talented. While we very much enjoyed the modern flare that Chef Rawal has put forth here, this menu clearly asks for a more traditional type of experience. Therefore, our vote is for Chef Mistry," Amar told them. "Chef Mistry will run the kitchen this week."

"Thank you, Chef," Karina said, not bothering to hide her smirk.

"Thank you, Chef," Aneel managed. One point for Karina. Three more weeks left.

Rakesh stood before them. "Chef Rawal will be the sous chef this round. We will be taking some footage as you cook this week for promo."

Aneel nodded, trying to hide his disappointment.

Sonny Pandya approached as they began cleanup and the camera crew shut down for the day. "I really love the modern touches you added. They were tasty and unique. Sometimes, though, people just want the food they remember from childhood. It wasn't your technique or your choices, it was the assignment."

Aneel thanked Sonny and turned to help clean up. His phone buzzed in his pocket. He pulled it out and glanced at the screen. His heart skipped a beat, and a wave of anger flooded through him.

His dad had texted. *I'd like to see you.*

Aneel swallowed and deleted the text. As if he would ever meet with his father. Yogesh Rawal hadn't been in his life since he was a child. His memories of the man were associated with the reek of alcohol and the sound of sobbing. Aneel inhaled deeply as he placed his phone back in his pocket and returned to the present.

"You'll have to come up with a menu for the week," he said to Karina.

"I already have it," Karina said, glancing at him. Her gaze settled on him for a moment, as if she saw something in his face.

Aneel adjusted his smirk, putting the text message in the

back of his mind. "Pretty confident about winning today, huh?"

"I like to be prepared." She paused as she looked at him. "You didn't make a weekly menu just in case?"

"Didn't want to jinx it," he replied.

"I consider making that menu a vote of confidence in myself. And if for whatever reason I don't get the win, I still have a great menu for the future, you know?"

"I consider it tempting fate."

Organization and planning had become Karina's friend.

She used to be spontaneous. Before her mother died when Karina was twenty and still in college. Rani had only been fifteen, and Sona was just graduating high school. The first year was the hardest. Their father was grief-stricken and spent all his time at the office, as if coming home was too hard. Karina had automatically moved home and commuted to her classes at University of Maryland. Someone had to be there for her sisters, so she'd been thrust into the role of parent. After all, they had lost their mother, too. Karina juggled college and dinner and schedules until Param's parents had seen enough and called her dad out. Thank goodness Param's parents were best friends with hers. Whatever they had said to her father, seemed to have awoken him. Because he started being more present after that.

If she hadn't been organized and prepared, no one would have eaten a proper dinner, and she would have failed out of school.

Those habits stayed with her, long after her father sought counseling and learned to manage his grief, becoming a parent again. Those habits ended up defining her. She graduated college and decided to go to culinary school, but she needed tuition money. She could have asked her father, but he had helped with her bachelor's degree, and she wanted to do this on her own.

After much searching, she ended up joining a competition advertised at their local culinary school.

That was where she had met Aneel.

"Still planning ahead, I see." Aneel held the door open for her as they walked to the back lot. The sun was still high, the air still warm, as if summer wanted to hang out in September. No matter. The fall chill, followed by winter, would be here soon enough. In the meantime, Karina raised her face to the warm sun.

"It's a way of life, not just something you do. So yes, seven years later, I'm pretty much the same person I was back then," she quipped. More or less.

"I did always admire that about you," he said as they walked to her car. He had donned sunglasses—aviators. Hers were in the bottom of her bag.

"Did you?" She squinted up at him. He was very tall.

He nodded. "I said as much, though you seem to have forgotten."

She had not forgotten. He had caught her practicing in one of the kitchens while everyone slept. It wasn't against the rules, but no one else seemed bothered enough to practice.

"Kind of late for lamb curry, isn't it, K?" Aneel popped his handsome head into the kitchen where she was intently trying something she had never done before.

She smiled at him. "Just practicing, A." She exaggerated the letter. Because she and Aneel had neighboring stations in the competition, they had started labeling their things in the fridge with their first initial. Aneel, of course, took it to the next level, addressing her only by her initial.

He entered the kitchen and stood on the outskirts of her station while she worked. He leaned against a counter, his hands in his pockets. "You've probably made that dish a hundred times."

She grinned and looked at him from under her lashes. "More."

"So you'll be fine." He leaned back on his arms, still looking at her face.

"I've never used this kind of cookware. I want to make sure the heat is proper," Karina insisted. She flushed as she took in his exposed muscular forearms and quickly looked away. She stirred the pot and inhaled. Smelled like she had done it correctly. "I like to be prepared for any problem."

He nodded. "That is impressive, admirable even." His eyes never left her face.

She flushed again under the intensity of his gaze. "Thanks. It works for me."

"Well, then." He stood, though he kept looking at her. "I'd offer to help, but—"

"It's against the rules." She rolled her eyes.

He nodded. "I'll leave you to it." He took a few steps, then stopped and turned back to her. "Smells like a winning dish, K."

"Well, it's been a long time." She opened her car door, threw her many bags over into the passenger seat and sat down. She looked up at him. "A lot has happened since that competition."

He lifted his sunglasses. His gaze ran over her face as if trying to read her, as if her face would reveal what the past seven years had brought. She put on her best poker face. It was none of his business what had happened to her.

"So it would seem." He stepped back and put his aviators back on.

She shut the door and pulled out of the lot. A glance in her rearview mirror found him still standing in the same spot.

Chapter Eight

It should bother him more that Karina won the first round. But Sonny's words had been encouraging, and it wasn't really about who won each week. It was about who the judges thought qualified for the job after four weeks of competition.

Karina was more organized, that was true. He was more fly by the seat of your pants. But only while cooking, not managing. He *had* made a menu for the week just in case. He just didn't want Karina to know. As much as he'd teased her about planning ahead, it was one of the things he had learned from her at that last competition. Though he'd never tell her that.

It was clear that Karina still maintained that she had been sabotaged in the last competition. Even though the investigation had determined no foul play, Karina had somehow maintained that the plug had been removed intentionally.

To be honest, he had no idea how that plug had come undone. Karina wasn't wrong in her assessment that the plug was heavy duty. Due to the set up of the area, it was on an extension cord, and it was possible the extension plug might have come loose. Either way, her dessert entry had melted. He had been as shocked as everyone else and had tried to offer his condolences, but Karina wasn't having it. Her anger had been palpable.

He could almost still feel the sharpness of her gaze as

she accused him. Aneel shook his head of the memory as he parked his car.

Saira was home when he got back to the apartment. She had her headphones on in front of her laptop, so he went directly to the bathroom to shower before hitting the kitchen. He needed to practice a few dishes.

He turned on old Bollywood songs from his grandparents' day that his mother used to play while she cooked. He had only ever met his grandparents a few times—trips to India did not come cheap, and they had passed away when he was a teenager. What he had noticed on one of those rare trips to India was that his grandmother played the same songs his mom did when she cooked. He would watch them bicker about recipes, trying new combinations, sometimes failing, sometimes not, those old songs playing in the background. His mom was always a bit melancholy upon returning to the States, but the songs remained.

The tradition had been wordlessly passed down. Those old songs were sappy and romantic, but they served the same purpose for him as they had for her. They made him feel close to his mother. Helped him focus.

He pulled out ingredients and pot and pans. He sharpened his knives and began the dance that was creation. He made food from his heart, not from a recipe. It never turned out quite the same twice, but it was always good. He was in the zone, humming along with the music and making food.

Then the music stopped.

He looked up. His sister was shaking her head at him. "What?"

"I've been trying to get your attention."

"Sorry. What's up?"

"I have to go in. To the lab."

"Here. Eat first." He ladled out some dhal and rice and placed the bowl in front of her on the small Formica table in

their tiny kitchen. They could have gotten a new one anytime, but this table had been in the kitchen they grew up in.
It reminded them of their mother, and they had both silently
agreed to keep it.

She dug in but then stopped two or three bites in.

"What?"

She shook her head. "Not as good as last time."

"I did the exact same thing." He tasted it. It *was* off.

"Clearly not. And how do you know that if you never write
anything down?" She looked at him, exasperated.

"I can fix it." He moved about the kitchen, adding to the
dhal.

"Honestly, Bhaiya. Write. Stuff. Down." She glared at him.
This was not the first time they'd had this conversation.

"That's not how Mom did it."

"Mom was a home cook. If she got it different, only you
and I knew. At work, she followed directions. You are trying
to be head chef. You are competing with Karina Mistry. *Who
writes everything down.*"

Aneel reached over and held his sister's hand. "I can handle Karina Mistry."

Saira squeezed his hand, a small smile on her lips. "Of
course you can. But you should still be more organized if
you're competing with her." Her phone buzzed next to her.
She grabbed for it, as if she didn't want him to see who was
contacting her.

"Who is texting you?" he asked.

"Lin," Saira said easily, refering to her closest friend in
veterinary school. But she didn't meet his eyes. "She needs
me at the clinic."

Aneel paused for a moment wondering what was going on
with her. "Everything okay? You're being vague."

"Bhaiya. I'm good. Lin is having…some issues and I'm
helping her."

He didn't believe her, but he knew he couldn't force it right now. And maybe Lin was having issues. He waved her off. "Go. Learn to be a vet."

She gathered her things and kissed him on the cheek. "Think about it."

He stared at the door after she left. She was right. He needed to have a consistent product if he was going to run a restaurant. He sighed as he opened his laptop and pulled up a new document. He turned the music back on and went back to work. This time taking notes.

The music took him back to his mother. His mom had died from cancer within one month of her diagnosis. She never visited the doctor, and by the time she eventually went to the hospital, the disease was everywhere. She had refused treatment.

Aneel had just turned twenty-five years old. Saira was just finishing high school. Just after her death, the songs had caused him and Saira heartache, they never played them. About a year later, he was cooking and his grief hit him hard as he tried to duplicate a sweet his mother had made. The silence was deafening, so he turned on the OG songs. The lilting memories and words made him feel like his mother was right there in the kitchen with him. As if she guided his hand. As if he hadn't lost her at all. Now he never cooked without her.

Aneel recalled the text from his father earlier in the day. It wasn't the first one. Though Aneel had not responded to any, his father still periodically sent a text. This had been happening over the last couple months.

Aneel inhaled to calm his irritation. Yogesh Rawal could text all he wanted, Aneel would never reply. His dad had come to the hospital before his mom died and offered to help. Aneel had turned him away. It was the first time Aneel had seen him in the fifteen years since he'd left. Aneel wanted nothing to do with him.

After his mother had passed, Aneel became Saira's guardian and promised his mother that he would get her a full higher education. By some stroke of luck, his father never pressed for custody of Saira, though Aneel lived in fear of it.

In the last few months, his father had been texting Aneel every so often, trying to reconnect, Aneel supposed. He didn't know, because he rarely read the messages.

Aneel had managed without a father. He had no reason to need a father now.

Chapter Nine

Karina drove home, a feeling of victory in her blood. She was ready to impress the judges this week with her menu and her ability to run that kitchen.

After the competition, the rest of her Monday was free. Which meant she could pick up Veer from school. She pulled up to the school and found Veer waiting in the pickup line with his teacher. His eyes lit up at the sight of her car, and joy filled her.

"Mom!" he called to her, practically shoving his Avengers backpack into the car as he climbed into the car seat. His teacher buckled him in and waved them off. "You came to pick me up!" Veer bounced with excitement.

"I got done early today."

"Can we have McDonald's?"

Karina inhaled. She was a professionally trained chef. Of course, her son wanted fast food. "Sure!"

"This is the best day. Ever," Veer announced from his seat. He then went on to tell her all about his day while she picked up McDonald's from the drive-through.

When they got home, her phone buzzed as she entered the front door. It was a text from a former catering client of hers, Mrs. Arora. Karina had informally catered from her home for extra money when she was in school and even before. Just small events to start, around ten people. She continued until she was promoted to head sous chef at Fusion. But every so often, Mrs Arora or one or two of her other regulars would request something. She could cook from her home, so she usually said yes.

Mrs. Arora needed catering for one hundred people this weekend. She'd just found out that her brother had planned nothing for his wife's milestone fiftieth birthday, so they were scrambling to plan a party. She was willing to pay quite a bit extra for the last-minute request.

Karina could really use the money. Not to mention, keeping a good relationship with her catering clients wouldn't hurt in case the head chef thing went to Aneel. She had to stay prepared. There was really no way to say no. Even though she had no idea how she was going to make this happen. Especially since now, she was head chef for the week. She was going to have to enlist a sister or two and maybe even Param and one of his brothers.

She FaceTimed her sister as she set out McDonald's for Veer. "Hey, Rani. Any chance you're free this week? To help me cook for a hundred people on Saturday."

"Sorry, Karina Ben. I'm on service for the rest of the week," Rani said. "Maybe Param can help?"

"I need to ask him to watch Veer." Karina really could not turn this down. "Maybe Sona is around?" She reached into the freezer for the Tater Tots. Yes, she was a chef, but her kid liked Tater Tots, and he wanted them with his McDonald's burger. Her hand grazed the familiar Ziploc bag with her mom's chai masala. She grabbed it and pulled it out. Seemed lighter. "Rani! Mom's masala—there's only like half left!" she nearly screamed into the phone.

Her sister looked unfazed.

"What do you know?" Karina demanded.

"Um, well. Papa uses it every once in a while, and she's been gone fifteen years, so..."

"But this is all we have of her." Karina shook her head. This wasn't happening.

"Karina Ben. It's okay—"

"No, it actually is not."

"Okay, fine. You tell Papa he can't use Mom's masala."

Karina glared at her sister. She would do no such thing. She could try to replicate it, but she had tried years ago, and it hadn't worked.

Rani shrugged. "Well?"

"Well, what?"

"Did you win?"

Karina shifted gears. She put the masala back into the back of the freezer. She'd deal with it later. "I did. Head chef for the week." She pulled out the Tater Tots. "And my menu is ready to go." At least as head chef, she wouldn't be doing much actual cooking this week. So she could work out a menu for Mrs. Arora's party.

Mrs. Arora had requested heavy apps. Karina could prep when she was home and execute Saturday before Fusion opened for dinner. She might not sleep much, but she could do this.

"I also need to find a pair of hands to help with this party."

"Call a friend," her baby sister said.

Karina stared at Rani. "What?"

"Call a friend."

Karina shook her head. She racked her brain for someone she could call that wasn't part of her family or Param's. She had no friends.

She texted her middle sister. No answer.

"Let me know if you hear from Sona. Where has she been anyway?" Karina asked.

"She's been busy with school and photography. She has weddings and parties. I've never seen her so dedicated to something," Rani said.

"Breaking up with Steve was good for her, then," Karina

said, grinning at her sister. Sona had been in one bad relationship after another. Well not bad, just not right…for her. This latest break-up had led to their middle sister applying herself to college and her passion like she never had before. It was a beautiful thing.

"So it would seem." Rani was walking around her house, taking care of housework, it seemed. "Tell me your menu for the week."

Karina told her.

"Ooh…these are classics. So yummy. The things that Mom used to make on special occasions."

Karina beamed and nodded. "You got it."

"Well, I have been home today, so I made dinner for you all," Rani announced.

Karina froze. "You what?" Her sister was an amazing pediatrician, a dedicated daughter and a wonderful sister, aunt and wife. What she was not, was a good cook.

Rani shook her head at her sister, amusement on her face. "Come on now. I played to my strengths."

"Unless that means you got Param to cook…"

Rani grinned. "I got us takeout. I'll be over around six."

Tuesday morning Karina awoke feeling happy and light. After all, she had won the first competition, and now she had a party to cater this weekend. Not to mention, she loved autumn.

And today was the most perfect autumn day for the start of Karina's week as head chef at Fusion. The air was crisp, the sun was bright and the leaves looked beautiful.

"Mom, you look like Captain Marvel today," Veer said as she buckled him up in the back seat.

"Do I?" she asked, an eyebrow raised. Captain Marvel was tall and blonde.

"Yes. You have a big smile on your face like she does when she knows she's going to get the bad guy," Veer said.

"Well, I guess I am feeling pretty powerful today." She smiled and kissed the top of his head.

Who wanted to think about emails from ex-husbands, or vexing competitors when she could almost smell the pie she could make for Veer from fresh fall apples?

A smile was plastered to her face as she arrived at the farmers market after taking Veer to school. Carlos had used a different market for his produce, but Karina had her own favorite. This was a bit out of the way, but worth it as far as she was concerned. Might as well run up two bills. One for Fusion and one for the party this weekend. She had come extra early so she could do all the shopping.

The market stretched the length and width of this particular parking lot, white tents for as long as the eye could see. Karina had discovered this place while in culinary school, and noticed that the chefs from her favorite local places shopped here. She had never been able to convince Carlos that the time and slight extra cost was worth it.

She grabbed her bags and headed first for the produce. She was intently choosing tomatoes and other vegetables when a familiar voice leaned into her.

"Who would have thought we used the same farmers market?" Aneel Rawal's deep purr was easily distinguished from any other voice she knew. Not to mention he always smelled like spice and leather.

Against everything she knew was rational, a slight thrill went through the area he had leaned towards. Vexing competitor indeed.

She turned, barely concealing her surprise. Even his little smirk could not change her mood today. "Well, who knew you had actual taste?" she purred right back. He was wearing a leather jacket against the fall chill, with a fitted black T-shirt and jeans.

Aneel tilted his head back and laughed, his mouth stretching into a huge smile on his clean shaven face that invoked not one but two incredibly attractive dimples. Hmm. She'd forgotten about those.

Her tomatoes chosen, she moved toward the onions, grabbing cucumbers on the way. Aneel kept pace with her, his bags empty in his hands.

"Why are you here?" she asked as she inspected a cucumber. "This is mostly a restaurant chef's haunt." She was keenly aware of his body close to hers as they shopped.

"I am a restaurant chef." He raised his eyebrows at her. He reached over her arm and picked up a cucumber. This placed her face right next to his broad chest, his scent filling the area around her, the heat from his body warming her. He quickly inspected the cucumber and handed it to her. She added it to the bag and stepped back.

"Oh, *right*." She looked up at him and smirked, even as she swallowed hard from his proximity. "I do keep forgetting that."

A small side smile on his face, dark eyes clearly amused, he appeared unfazed by her ribbing.

"Well, I love this place and I find the quality here superior. I was going to bring some produce to the restaurant to prove it to you." He pressed his lips together and dropped his gaze. "I suppose I wrongly assumed you would just use the place Carlos liked."

"Ha," she guffawed. "I suppose I'm smarter than you anticipated."

"Not at all." His voice softened. "I always knew how smart you are." Something flickered in the warmth of his brown eyes.

Whether it was his words, or the way he was looking at her, Karina was speechless for a moment. Silence drifted between them.

"You're just more worldly than I gave you credit for." He chuckled and the spell was broken.

Karina continued her search for vegetables, her bags filling up. Aneel continued to chatter beside her, every so often leaning over and grabbing produce to add to what was now, their bag. He talked about the different vegetables, and how he chose them. He offered his bags when hers filled. Begrudgingly, Karina had to admit to herself that he was quite knowledgeable, and she learned a few things from him. She was surprised that she felt no resentment, and even found herself laughing a few times.

Must just be the beautiful fall day.

They finished with the vegetables and herbs and headed for the meat section.

"What is your sister up to?" Karina asked.

Aneel stared at her a moment.

"You have a sister, right?" She could have sworn a young woman who was his sister had stopped by the competition a few times.

"I do. I just didn't think you would remember." He was genuinely surprised. He paused as if trying to puzzle her out. "She's fine. She's in vet school."

"That's great. Good for her," Karina responded. The way he was looking at her made her flush so she turned her attention to the meats.

"Have you ever cooked with the meats from here?"

His face lit up. "Of course. Such great cuts, it's almost impossible to mess it up in the kitchen."

She grinned at him. "Well, *I* can't. Don't know about you."

He rolled his eyes but followed her. "Don't you worry about me. I can hold my own in the competition." His tone was light, but Karina was suddenly reminded that he was not her friend. He was what stood between her and the future she needed.

She turned to face him straight on, all amusement gone from her. "Maybe you can. Doesn't mean you'll win."

Chapter Ten

The week was flying by. Karina was trying to spend time with Veer, to make sure he was adjusting to the new school year, as well as lead the kitchen all at the same time. She had received two more emails from Chirag this week. She had replied to none of them.

She couldn't possibly imagine seeing him after all these years. Or what he could say to her that could put things right. Besides, she hardly had the time to deal with him right now.

Still…was she wrong, keeping Veer from meeting his father?

She shook the thought away. She'd think about it later.

"How was school today?" she asked her son as she put apples and peanut butter in front of him for a snack. She had been able to sneak out of the restaurant for a bit to pick him up from early dismissal.

"Great," he said, moving his whole body as he dipped an apple slice into the peanut butter.

"Tell me one thing you talked about in circle time." She began prepping pie crust for mini pies for the party. Might as well get some work done while she was chatting.

"Families."

"Yeah? What about families?"

"Like some have two moms, some have two dads, some have one mom or one dad. Some have one mom and one dad. Blah blah." He bit into his apple slice.

"Blah blah?" She grinned at him as she started slicing fruit for the pies.

He shrugged. "Is Param Mama my dad?"

Karina nearly cut herself chopping. "What? Why would you say that?"

Veer swallowed and then counted on his fingers. "He's a boy. He makes me food. He plays with me. He loves me. He loves you. I love him." He held up six sticky fingers to her as proof that Param could be his dad.

"All true. But Param is your uncle, that's why you call him Param Mama."

Veer looked at her and nodded, accepting her answer. "Do I have a dad? Or are we a family with just a mom?"

She couldn't lie to him. Her mind drifted back again to the latest emails from Chirag.

"It would be fun to have a dad, I think," he said.

"Oh yeah? Why?"

He counted on his fingers again. "Because he would be a boy, like me. And Julie has a mom and a dad, and they always do fun things together."

"Like what?" She started the stove to precook some of the sliced apples for the pie filing. The warm aroma of cinnamon started to fill the air.

"Like they go bowling. Or swimming. Or ice skating."

"We do that, you and me," she said to him. "Or Param Mama takes you or Sona Masi. Even Dada takes you places."

He rolled his eyes. "Dada takes me to the bookstore."

"The bookstore is fun," Karina insisted with a smile. "He reads you a story and gets you treats. That's what grandfathers do."

He grinned. "Dada does all the voices. And he always buys me a cookie."

She watched her sweet boy eat the apple and peanut butter. He was making a sticky mess, but his intensity was real.

No, she would not be telling Veer about Chirag. But it seemed she may have to meet with him. At the very least, she was going to have to answer his emails at some point. She put the thought out of her mind. She'd deal with it later.

"Well? Do I have a dad?" Veer looked at her, innocent eyes wide with the question.

Veer was happy here. He had great role models in this family. Karina was torn between lying to her son and protecting him. What was worse? Telling him he did not have a dad or telling him he did have a father, but he had chosen not to be around? That she didn't trust the man?

"What you have is this whole family and Param Mama's whole family who all love you and are always going to be here for you," she punted.

Veer's face fell a bit.

"What?"

He shrugged. "I love everyone. But I think it would have been nice to have a dad."

Karina's phone twittered, a notification that someone was at the mudroom door. She had the camera set for motion. Veer grabbed her phone with his peanut butter hands. She cringed.

"Dada is here!" he said, dropping her phone. She picked it up and was wiping it as her father walked in the door, bringing the chill with him.

"Where is my favorite grandson?" her father called from the mudroom.

Veer giggled. "Dada. I'm your only grandson."

"Still my favorite." Her father came into the kitchen and sat down next to Veer.

"Papa. Mrs. Arora has asked me to cater a last-minute party for this Saturday."

"Uh-huh?" Her father eyed her.

"Any chance I get you to help?"

"How about I watch Veer and Param or Sona can help you?"

She grinned. "Deal."

"Dada. Let's go to the bookstore!" Veer gave his grandfather his biggest smile.

"I was hoping you would ask." He looked at his daughter.

She nodded. "I need to work on a menu for this party before I go back to the restaurant. That would be great." She sighed. She had her village. Veer was happy. They did not need Chirag's complications.

Luckily, Aneel was quite talented and not at all a sore loser, and he did everything she asked in the kitchen and more. It was as if he knew she had other things on her mind and seamlessly helped her make the kitchen flow. The past few days flew by in a whirlwind of shopping at the market, dealing with members of the staff being out sick and paperwork. Aneel picked up any slack in the kitchen, including washing dishes. Most sous chefs she knew wouldn't touch the dishes.

Still, she found it harder to unwind at the end of the day and tossed and turned late into the night, in anticipation of the next day and what it might bring. Rather than feeling like she was killing it during her week as head chef, she felt like she was just barely treading water. Not to mention, it was Thursday, and she still hadn't heard from Sona, who was her last bastion of hope. Param, it turned out, had play performances with his seventh graders all weekend. Rani, of course, was busy in the emergency department. If Sona flaked, Karina would be catering for a hundred people all by herself.

Sona ended up coming to the restaurant Thursday afternoon.

"Hey. Where have you been?" Karina asked Sona, one eye still on her kitchen.

Sona beamed. "My photography has really taken off since Rani's wedding." She sighed as she put down her bag. "I can't stay, I was in the neighborhood taking some pictures for class, thought I'd stop by, since I haven't been able to respond to your texts. What's up?"

"I need an extra pair of hands for the next couple days. Mrs. Arora has a last-minute party she wants me to cater for her. A hundred people, but I've been here all week. I've gotten things started, and she has hired day-of help, but I still have to cook. She's paying almost double."

"First." Her sister grinned at her. "That's amazing! Second, if I can, I'll stop over between gigs. But as of right now, I have a bunch of parties to photograph this weekend. In fact, that may be one of them." She scrolled on her phone. "It is. I'll see what I—" Sona glanced behind Karina and gave a small smirk. "Who is this?"

"Chef?" Aneel called from behind as she heard him approach.

Karina turned. Aneel was walking toward her, whites unbuttoned, sleeves rolled up. A common look for him predinner service. One that she didn't mind at all. "Yes."

"We...ah...need you in the back." He glanced at Sona. "Hi, I'm Aneel. You must be her sister."

"How can you tell?" Sona asked, the tease obvious in her voice. Karina glared at her sister.

"You're both..." He flushed as if he was embarrassed. "You look alike."

Sona maintained her smirk as if she knew what Aneel had been about to say. "We get that a lot."

Karina rolled her eyes. "I need to go." She tilted her head toward the kitchen. "Have you eaten?"

"No. But I'll be late for class."

"I can pack you something to go," Aneel offered.

"That would be great." She smiled at him.

Karina narrowed her eyes at her sister. Sona was easily the prettiest of the three of them, and she was openly flirting with Aneel. Not that it bothered Karina. Sona could do what she wanted. As could Aneel.

"I'm really sorry I can't be your sous chef, Karina Ben," Sona said to Karina.

"No problem. I'll figure it out. Wait a moment, I'll send food out." Karina hugged her sister and went back to the kitchen with Aneel at her side.

"What's the problem?" she asked him as they walked.

"The fish you ordered did not come. I sent Camille to the fish market. We should be okay, but maybe running a few minutes behind. Stacy has the fish vendor on the phone for you. I'll get food for your sister."

Karina just stared at him. Wow. Impressive. "Thank you." She started to walk away to deal with the fish vendor.

"Um. Why did you need your sister to be your sous chef?" Aneel asked, eyebrows raised. "That's my job." He pursed his lips. "Well, at least this week."

Karina shook her head. "Oh no. Not for here. It's... I got a last-minute catering job from a regular client for a party this weekend, and I need an extra pair of hands." She paused. She really did not want to ask him, but he was more than competent, and she was getting desperate. She frowned at him. "I don't suppose you're available when you're not here?"

Aneel shrugged. "Sure. I'd be happy to. Just text me the location and times."

"I can pay you. Not as much as you get here, but she pays me well, and she pays in cash."

"Okay. That sounds fine."

"Really?" Relief was already flooding her. With Aneel's help, she was guaranteed to deliver quality on time and still manage things here.

Aneel smiled as he nodded. "Yes. Why do you look so surprised?"

Her mouth gaped open. "I just didn't expect...usually my family—"

"Well, I'm happy to help." The look on his face... He wasn't being snarky, he truly had no other agenda. Hmm. "It's been an exceptionally crazy week here. I had no idea you were also juggling a catering job." When she did not move, Aneel nodded toward the office. "The fish guy..."

"Right." She grinned at him, a great weight off her chest, and walked toward the office. She stopped and turned back to him. "Thank you."

Chapter Eleven

Aneel was exhausted. Being sous chef felt like head chef without the prestige or paycheck. And now he had volunteered to spend his "free time" helping Karina cater. Not volunteered. He was getting paid. That was why he was helping her—because he needed the money. Not because he wanted to help her.

He preferred to ignore the fact that he blurted out his yes before he knew there was money involved.

The sun had just risen, the sky filled with oranges and pinks turning into yellow. The light helped to wake him up. The plan was to work on the catering until they had to go into the restaurant later this afternoon. That gave them close to eight hours. He checked the address Karina had texted him and looked out the window of his car. Seemed right. But he was looking at a single-family home. A house. She was cooking at her *house*.

He walked up and rang the doorbell and was greeted by an older man with Karina's eyes and smile. He had a crossbody bag on one shoulder and a to-go mug in the other. Aneel smelled chai.

"Hello," the older man said. "I am Sachin, Karina's dad. I'd shake your hand, but…" He smiled, and it was Karina's smile. "My hands are full. She's expecting you. Come on in."

"Nice to meet you, Uncle," Aneel said as he stepped into the house. "Aneel Rawal."

Sachin Mistry eyed him for a moment. "Well. Thanks for coming. Karina is quite stressed. The family appreciates you helping her." His eyes widened as he glanced behind him at the kitchen and cleared his throat. "Good luck." The older man was out the door in a flash.

Aneel easily found his way to the large open kitchen. It was organized chaos, with Karina in the middle of it. Her hair was up in a tight ponytail, she had on a loose fitting T-shirt and leggings, and her face was without makeup. Her lips were moving as if she were talking to someone or singing. But he did not see earbuds in her ears.

Years ago in that last competition, he had paused—just like this—to watch her. A natural beauty in her element, he had thought. His heart had thudded in his twenty-seven-year-old chest. She had caught him looking and glared at him, and he had offered an apology for staring. But the reality was he had been completely taken by her.

"You're beautiful," he said to her, his youth making him bold and free.

She shook her head at him like he was crazy, tucking a stray hair behind her ear and flushing at his compliment. The flush only served to make her more beautiful.

Some things didn't change.

She was chopping an onion while oil heated in a pan on the stove. A round spice container was sitting in front of her. Still her lips moved as if in conversation.

"Good morning," he said, so she would know he was there.

She startled as she looked up at him. "Hi." She nodded over her shoulder. "Sink is over there, and there should be an extra apron in this drawer."

"Okay." He quickly washed up and tied on the apron. "Who were you talking to?"

She narrowed her eyes at him. "I wasn't talking to anyone."

"Your lips were moving."

"They were not." She furrowed her brow, clearly indignant.

He raised his eyebrows at her. "You most certainly were. I saw you moving your lips as you chopped onions."

She narrowed her eyes at him. "You were watching me?"

Busted. He stared at her. "No." Denial was the right move here, but he shifted his gaze away from her penetrating stare. "I just noticed as I walked in. What are we making?" Better to get right to work here. He was no longer young enough to be bold and free.

Karina sprinkled cumin seeds into the pan with oil and filled him in on the menu. It was heavy hors d'oeuvres, no main meal. But many of the hors d'oeuvres would be passed on trays, and therefore needed to be bite-size.

"Okay. Got it. You cook, and I'll assemble. I assume you have a large fridge?"

Karina nodded toward a small hallway. "Through the mudroom to the garage. Dedicated to this party. They hired staff to come pick up on Saturday before we leave for work."

"Well, we better get moving." They only had today and tomorrow—and they both had to be at Fusion by 4:00 p.m. for dinner service. He immediately got to work assembling the small pies in front of him. He could have sworn Karina stopped and stared at him for a minute.

"Those will be half-baked. Their staff will finish them off at the event Saturday night," Karina said.

"Makes sense," he said. "Your client must really like your food, to pay double and pay for extra staff."

"Mrs. Arora was one of my first ever clients when I needed work. I like to make her happy." She shrugged. "Do you mind if I turn on some music?"

"Nope."

Karina washed her hands and picked up her phone. She tapped a few times and old Bollywood songs drifted out from a speaker in the kitchen.

Aneel stopped and smiled at her. "OG Bollywood, huh?"

"My mom—"

"Always played it when she cooked." He grinned. "Mine, too. I play it all the time when I cook. Sets the mood. My sister likes to tease me about it. She'd die if she knew someone else did the same thing." Truth was, Saira would have a cow if she knew that Aneel was helping Karina Mistry cook.

She just stared at him. "Did you learn from your mom?"

He nodded. "All the basics. She was a line cook as long as I can remember. She worked in local restaurants." He shrugged. "The hours were long, but it paid. She taught me so I could feed me and my sister when she worked."

"What about your dad?"

It was an innocent question. Normal, in fact, to ask. Aneel pressed his lips together. "He wasn't around."

"Oh. I'm sorry." Karina glanced at him and moved on. "So then, cooking is in your blood." He heard the forced lightness as she tried to move away from her unwitting question about his dad. "I used to always be in the kitchen when my mom was cooking. She and my dad were pediatricians. They worked together. Well, my dad still… is a pediatrician." She paused. "So anyway, she didn't cook every day. But whenever she did, I would drop everything and come help."

They just looked at each other for a moment, sharing the fact that they had both learned to cook from their moms. And that they had both lost them.

"I remember you telling me that your mom had passed—cancer, right?" Karina said.

He nodded. "You lost yours in a car accident?"

"You remember."

"Hard to forget," he said softly.

"It's a weird club, for sure," she answered. "I was talking to my mom. Before. When you came in." She met his gaze.

He nodded. "Yeah. I get that."

They worked in companionable silence for a bit.

"Your sister is a photographer?" he asked.

"We don't have to do that, you know," Karina said.

"Do what?" The mini pies were almost done. Samosas next.

"Make conversation because it's just the two of us."

"I like talking to you." He had since the day he met her seven years ago.

"You chat up everybody in the kitchen. Like you can't stop talking," she said, matter-of-fact. "Besides, I'm your boss."

"I like getting to know people. And you might be my boss, but that's just for this week." He chuckled.

"Get used to it," she snarked at him, but a smile played at her lips. "And constant drivel is distracting."

"It's not drivel." He chuckled. "And don't worry, you'll get to be my sous chef next week."

"You think you're going to win on Monday?" she asked.

"I am sure of it." He glanced up at her from his task.

"Really?" Her eyebrows shot up. He wasn't sure if in challenge or surprise.

"Really." He nodded. "You cook differently than you did before. You take less risk."

"All you do is smash different things together and see if it's edible."

"It's not quite that crass, but okay." He gave a one-shoulder shrug. "You never know when you'll find that perfect combo of flavor that hits just perfectly."

"I like knowing what the end result will be."

"We all know that about you."

She gasped not at his words, but at what he was doing. "That is not how you wrap a samosa!" she exclaimed.

"It's not how *you* wrap a samosa, but it is how *I* do it," he countered. He was making the triangle, of course, but folded differently than she did.

"It'll come apart in the oil," she warned.

"No, it won't."

"It's wrong." She stayed firm.

"It's *different*."

She rolled her eyes and turned away from him.

"So, two sisters and your dad, and no one would help you?" he said, his voice dripping with sarcasm. "Can't imagine why."

"They're busy." She shrugged.

"You're particular," he said to her.

"How did you know all about my family?" She narrowed her eyes at him.

"Well, I met some, and…" He paused. "And I remember," he added, his voice quiet. They had enjoyed more than one late-night chat when they'd been too keyed up to sleep.

She snapped her head to him and held his gaze. *She remembered.*

"Mommy," a small gravelly voice called out.

Aneel's turn to snap his head around.

Karina dropped everything, wiping her hands on her apron as she went toward the sound of that voice.

A little boy, maybe four years old, sporting Captain America pajamas, unruly dark hair and the same shade of beautiful brown skin as Karina, shuffled into the kitchen. He rubbed his eyes and yawned.

And it tugged at Aneel's heart. The action recalled memories of Saira about that age doing the same thing. But she used to call for him since their mother was usually working.

"Jai Shri Krishna, sweetie." Karina got down on her knees in front of the boy.

"Jai Shri Krishna," the boy said on a yawn and fell into Karina's arms.

"Where's Sona Masi?" Karina asked.

"Brushing her teeth," the boy said from her shoulder. "I need to defrost."

Karina smiled. "Of course. Let's go." Her voice was soft and sweet and full of love. A pleasure to listen to. She stood, the boy in her arms, and turned to Aneel. "I'll just be a minute until Sona comes down."

Aneel nodded, still in a bit of shock. "Yeah. Sure. I'll just be here, wrapping samosas."

This earned him an eye roll and a smile. He watched her carry the boy out to the great room and sit down on the sofa, still holding him. She turned on a children's program, and the little boy shifted so he could see the TV. Karina wrapped a blanket around them.

Aneel watched them while he wrapped samosas, still trying to process what he was looking at.

Karina Mistry had a son.

Chapter Twelve

Karina focused on Veer, ignoring the look of pure surprise on Aneel's face. From the corner of her eye, she could see him wrapping samosas. *His way.* Sona would be down in a few minutes, and Karina would go back to work. But right now, she was in bliss. Just her and Veer watching *Blue's Clues*.

Mild clanging from the kitchen had her turning to see what was happening.

Aneel caught her gaze. "Sorry. Just looking for the—" He made a motion with his large hands to indicate the large deep pan she used for frying.

"In the cupboard under the stove," she said softly.

He found it and poured oil into it, prepping to par-fry the samosas. She nodded and turned back to Veer. She hadn't meant for Veer to meet Aneel. She was particular about who she let into her life and who got to see Veer. Pretty much no one did either. Though Aneel was just a colleague. He would be gone after tomorrow. A blip in Veer's timeline.

Sona emerged shortly after, squeezing Karina's shoulder in greeting as she passed by, heading straight for the kitchen.

"Good morning," she said brightly to Aneel.

Karina couldn't help it. She turned to watch Sona set water to boil for her morning chai. Everyone in her family drank chai. Except for her.

"Good morning, Sona," Aneel said, friendly as always.

"You remember my name," Sona said sweetly. Karina watched her lean against the island where Aneel was working, waiting for the water to simmer. She was flirting with him.

Something ugly twisted inside Karina. Why should she care? Sona could flirt with Aneel. Karina had no claim on him. She turned back to the show. She could hear them chatting but not what they were saying. Every so often, Sona would giggle. That something ugly in Karina took hold and grew.

Then she heard the freezer door open, so Karina looked back to the kitchen again. Sona had taken out their mother's chai masala.

"What are you doing?" Karina called from the sofa, not bothering to hide her horror.

"I'm making chai." Sona shrugged and looked at Karina like she was ridiculous.

"That's mom's masala," she hissed.

Sona widened her eyes, mocking her as she hissed back, "I know. We're out of the store-bought stuff."

"You can't use that," Karina continued to hiss. She vaguely noticed Aneel watching them as he silently fried samosa.

"Why not?" Sona asked even as she sprinkled some into her pot.

Defeated, Karina simply shook her head. "Because when it's gone…it's gone." She turned back to Josh and Blue and the current clues.

Sona continued chatting softly with Aneel, but Karina could not be bothered to care. After a few minutes, the aroma of the chai—and her mother's masala—floated over to her. Nothing smelled like this. This was a warm blanket on a cold day, a hug when you were sad, a mother's hand on your forehead.

And it would soon be gone.

"Sona," Karina called out, her voice stern to hide the tears that burned. "I really need to get back to work. Veer is ready for you."

Sona turned to her. "You got it." She walked over, her smirk disappearing when she saw Karina's face. "Is it the masala? I thought you were replicating it."

Karina shook her head, her mouth pressed together. "It's not coming out right."

Sona glanced at her mug of chai. "Sorry."

"It's fine." Karina forced a smile as she stood. "Enjoy the chai."

"You…" Sona looked at her pointedly "…enjoy your *cooking*."

Karina rolled her eyes at her sister. "I just need to get the work done."

Sona raised an eyebrow, a knowing smile on her face. "Uh-huh."

"Mind getting Veer dressed? Param will be here soon."

"Happy to leave you alone with your 'competition.'" Sona wiggled her eyebrows.

Karina flushed, even though there was no logical reason for it. Sure, she had found Aneel attractive when they were in that competition together. But all the women had, regardless of age. Karina and Aneel might have even flirted off and on; their stations had been next to each other after all. But nothing had ever happened between them during the competition. It was an unspoken rule that whatever might happen would happen after they finished the competition.

Once Karina believed that Aneel had cheated, she lost interest. And that was the end of that.

Until he showed up last week.

Of course now, he was after her job. He was still attractive, maybe even more so, but she didn't have time for all that. Sona could give her all the knowing looks she wanted, Karina was not going to pursue Aneel.

Karina joined the man in question in her kitchen. She let him deal with the samosas while she marinated the chicken.

"Your sister is sweet."

"Is she?" Her words came out harsher than she wanted, and she felt Aneel turn to her.

"Yes. She kept telling me what a great chef and mom you are."

Karina stilled and smiled. "Did she?"

"Yes. I think she was hoping I would back out simply from fear." He chuckled.

Karina allowed herself a laugh and turned to face him. "Did it work?"

Aneel met her gaze, his brown eyes taunting. "Almost. Then you called her away."

Karina froze. He couldn't possibly know what green and ugly thing had twisted inside her.

They worked in silence for a few minutes until Karina noticed that Sona had left the masala out. Karina rolled her eyes and tightly zipped the three layers closed and returned the bag to the back of the freezer. Rani probably used it, too, when Karina wasn't looking.

"That chai masala?" Aneel hedged. "Your mom made it?"

"Yes." It was all Karina could manage, all she wanted to say about it. She felt him glance at her and braced herself for more questions, but he simply went back to frying samosas.

Just then the mudroom door opened, and a loud but familiar voice boomed. "Hi, all!" Param called. He entered the kitchen and gave Karina a quick hug before turning to Aneel. He extended a hand. "Hi, I'm Param." He grinned at Karina. "I got to say, it's been a long time since Karina has had a sleepover."

Karina heated in a flash. "Param Sheth." She smacked his hand away. "What the hell are you saying?" She caught Aneel in her side view and found that he was flushed as well. "This is Aneel Rawal. We work together."

"But it's so early—"

"He's helping me with catering." She smacked her brother-in-law's shoulder again.

He held up two hands in defense. "Okay. Okay. Sorry. It's a legit assumption."

"It absolutely is not." She raised a hand again, but Param dodged and managed to extend his hand again to Aneel. "Param Sheth. I'm married to Rani, her youngest sister."

Aneel's face, while still slightly flushed, held amusement. He shook Param's hand. "Nice to meet you. I tease my sister, too." He chuckled.

Karina watched this exchange. No. No. No. She did not want her family getting comfortable with the enemy. "Aneel is also up for the executive chef position at Fusion," she offered, trying to let Param know he should not be friendly with Aneel.

"Oh yeah?" Param offered. "Oh, I see. You're competing against each other on that reality show." He sighed and shook his head at Aneel. "Good luck. You'll need it. Karina is the best."

There was that loyalty.

"She's amazing," Aneel agreed. "I clearly have my work cut out for me."

"Hi, Uncle." Veer had entered the kitchen unnoticed by anyone. He peered up at Aneel and waved.

"Hi...uh."

"Veer." Karina almost chuckled at Aneel's obvious surprise. "My son."

"Yeah." Aneel met her gaze. "I gathered that."

Karina expected him to return to the samosas, but to her surprise, he wiped his hands, turned off the oil and got on his knees in front of Veer and extended a hand. "Veer, I'm Aneel Uncle. It's nice to meet you. Love the Captain America T-shirt."

Veer grinned and shook Aneel's hand. Karina glanced at Param, who shot her a proud look. They had been practicing. "He's the best Avenger," Veer stated.

Aneel raised his eyebrows. "Is he, though? Because I kind of think that Iron Man is hands down the best Avenger."

Veer's eyes opened in horror. "He can't be. He is mean sometimes. Captain America is always nice."

"But Iron Man has all the lasers, and he's extra smart."

"But Captain America is also smart, and he has honor. Iron Man peed in his suit. On purpose!" Veer's negative opinion of this was clear.

Aneel smiled at Veer. "We'll have to agree to disagree."

"What does that mean?"

"That means we both agree that we could both be right," Aneel said.

Veer eyed him like this was a ridiculous thing, but he shrugged. "Are you a chef like my mom?"

"Yes. We…ah, work together."

"You're the idiot trying to get her job," Veer said as he glanced at his mother.

Before Karina could say anything, Aneel looked Veer in the eye and said, "I am that idiot."

Veer looked him over. "You don't seem crazy and mean and—"

"Okay." Karina put her hands on her son's shoulders and directed him toward the island. "Veer. Come on. What do you want for breakfast? Param Mama is taking you to school in a few."

"Param Mama!" Veer threw himself at Param's legs. Param easily lifted the boy and went about getting the child his cereal and milk.

Karina shook her head. She was never going to get Veer to change how he addressed Param.

"We'll eat at the sofa," Param said. "Since you have taken over the kitchen."

Veer and Param had breakfast together, then Veer kissed his mom before Param took him to school.

"Aneel Uncle, will you be here when I get home from school?" Veer asked him.

Aneel looked at Karina. She shook her head. "Probably not. We'll be at the restaurant."

"Bummer. We need to disagree more," Veer said. "Bye."

"He's great," Aneel said as soon as Veer and Param had left. "I meant Veer. Although your brother-in-law seems great, too." Wow, he was an idiot.

Karina looked at him, something wary in her eyes. "Thanks."

"You didn't mention that you had a son." He had been thrown for a second, but he was instantly enamored with the child. He now knew what Karina had been up to since that last competition.

"Well, we're not exactly friends, we're competitors. And I don't really talk about him outside of our family." Karina's voice was clipped, as if even talking about Veer needed a wall.

Aneel nodded as he waited for the oil to heat up again. "Protective. I totally get that."

"Good. As long as we understand each other."

"So where's his dad?" Aneel was prying. He knew it, but he had to know. He dropped a small piece of samosa crust into the oil. It sank a bit but bubbled right up.

Karina laughed. "Wow. You don't hold back."

He shrugged. "We're here. We're cooking. I just met your son. You clearly live here with your family, and you haven't once mentioned a husband or boyfriend." He turned to look at her, but her back was to him. "We were friends, at one time," he said quietly. He slowly started slipping samosas into the hot oil.

"Were we?" she asked quietly.

"We used to hang out, talk recipes. You told me about your mom." He paused. "I told you about mine. So yes, we shared things that were important to us, and we had fun and things in common. We were friends."

"What does that matter when you ended up cheating to win?"

Honestly. Anger rose up in him like fire. She was never going to let it go. What had he been thinking? That they could be friends? No, he'd been thinking that he was attracted to her. Well, that wasn't enough. "You know what," he said harshly, "I'm not going to keep defending myself against something you will never believe. I did not cheat," he growled at her. "There was an investigation."

"Then how did you win?" Karina narrowed her eyes at him.

"I won because you and I were tied. And my dessert was better," Aneel snapped.

"Your dessert did not melt," Karina snapped back.

"You're assuming you would have won if it hadn't melted."

"Well, we'll never know, now will we?" She sounded like a child on the playground.

"No, Karina. We won't. That's just how it is." Now *he* sounded like a child on the playground. He inhaled and exhaled. "The thirty K? I invested most of it so I could send my sister to school. The rest I used to rent us a slightly better apartment with a gas stove in the kitchen." It was more than he had planned to share. Maybe he should not have said anything. Too late now.

Karina just stared at him, speechless. That was a first. Then she furrowed her brow. "You didn't use it for culinary school?" she asked, genuine surprise in her voice.

He shook his head, still seething at her.

"How did you learn how to do all this?"

"I taught myself. YouTube, books. I asked a million questions of the chefs at Chutney Catering while I cleaned their messes and did their dishes."

"They must have loved that." She raised her eyebrows, a small smile working at her mouth.

He let out a breath. "They did not in fact love that. But I needed to learn."

"Chutney Catering had some old-school chefs there," she mused.

He nodded. "They knew all the technical stuff, but they simply did not move forward with their cuisine. I learned what I could, and then I applied it to what I wanted to do."

"Impressive," she said softly.

"Wait. Was that a *compliment* I heard from Karina Mistry?" He put his hand over his heart.

A smile came to her mouth, despite her obvious efforts to squish it. "Don't kill a smile, Karina. You never know when another will come your way."

She rolled her eyes, which let the smile out. "Divorced," she said at last on a sigh.

Aneel went completely still. Almost as if, if he moved, she would stop talking.

"Veer's dad and I were very briefly married. He went to Nepal to 'find himself' before Veer was born and didn't return." She lifted her chin, defiant. "So I divorced him. He has never even seen Veer." Her tone that indicated that she didn't really care, that she was fine, but he could see she was anything but.

"Well. His loss. I can tell from my ten-minute interaction with Veer that he's a pretty amazing boy. Most likely because of you and your family."

She flushed. "Thanks. For saying that."

"I meant it."

"It doesn't mean we're friends," she said quickly.

"Of course not," he said just as quickly. "We don't want any friendships forming here. We are competitors, and competitors only. This is a friendship-free zone."

She smiled faintly at him. "As long as we understand each other."

The time passed quickly as she and Aneel worked side by side. She had been right. Working with Aneel was definitely more efficient than working with her sisters, or even Param. Before she knew it, the mudroom door had opened, and Veer came barreling through.

"Mommy, Mommy. Mommy. Guess what I did in school today?" He came into the kitchen and stopped as he saw Aneel still there working, helping her clean up before they left for the restaurant. "Hey, Aneel Uncle, you said you might not be here!"

"Well, I guess I got lucky because I get to see you again," Aneel answered amiably.

"You wanna see what I did today in school?" Veer asked him.

Karina was about to let Aneel off the hook, when he met her eyes and silently asked for permission. Which blew her away. She nodded, smiling softly.

"I would love to." Aneel turned to Veer. "What did you do?" He stopped what he was doing and sat down cross-legged on the floor next to Veer. Her son was more than happy to empty the contents of his backpack and show Aneel Uncle exactly what he had been doing at school today.

To his credit, Aneel was a great sport, showing what appeared to be real interest in the letter *H*, the number *5* and everything else. Though she tried her best to fight it, she was touched.

"Veer. I need you to go with Param Masa in the other room, and he'll bring you a snack."

"Param *Mama*." Veer nodded and melted again into Param's legs. "Aneel Uncle, maybe you need to watch the Avenger movies again, and then you can see why Captain America is the best."

"As soon as I can, I'll watch Captain America again."

Veer's eyes widened. "Seriously?"

"Of course."

Karina had heard enough. "Veer. Go with Param Masa. I'm coming."

Veer allowed himself to be guided out of the kitchen, but not before he mumbled, "Param Mama."

Aneel stood and washed his hands before returning to work. "What's that all about?"

Karina sighed. "Our family and Param's family are super close. So when Veer was born, I had him address Param and his brothers as if they were my brothers, too. 'Mama'. But Param just married my sister, which makes him 'Masa'." She shook her head. "I'm about to just give up trying to change it."

"The love is real. Between Veer and Param. And you and Param. Why change it because your sister got married?" Aneel said softly, leaning against the counter.

Karina rested her gaze on him. He was definitely more observant than she was comfortable with. "You don't have to watch the movie again."

Aneel nodded. "I wasn't going to."

"Oh." Karina was taken aback. So he had just flat out lied to her son.

"I don't need to. I always have them on at my house. I know the lines by heart." He grinned from ear to ear, clearly proud of himself. As proud as any little boy would be.

Karina stared at him. "You mean, this is not a phase for him? He's going to talk about this...for the rest of his life?" A slight panic slid through her body.

Aneel shrugged. "Hey, I don't know about all that. I just speak for myself."

Karina shook her head. "We have to go. We'll be late." She

went to Veer on the sofa and kissed him goodbye. "Thanks, Param."

"No problem," he said, distracted by the TV. *Iron Man* was on.

Oh god.

Chapter Thirteen

Aneel thoroughly enjoyed peppering Karina with questions about her family and her son. He continued to do so whenever they had a private moment all through dinner service. Dinner dragged a bit longer tonight, and Aneel heard Karina groan to herself.

"What's the matter, *executive chef*, too much for you?" He elbowed her and smiled.

"No, I just need to get more of that catering prep done tonight." She inhaled. "Not sure what I was thinking when I said yes to Mrs. Arora."

"Listen, I can handle things here, close up and all that, if you want to go home a bit early and work."

"Seriously? You'd do that?" She eyed him suspiciously.

"I'll try not to steal the position from you today," he said with a slight eye roll.

She gave him that blank stare that consistently unnerved him. "As if." She smirked.

"Go. Before I change my mind." He nodded at the back door.

Karina grabbed her things and left.

Aneel dealt with the staff and the cleanup, making sure all was ready for tomorrow before he finally left. Two hours later, he pulled up in front of Karina's house, the kitchen light still on, just as he had expected.

He picked up his phone to text her, first deleting the most recent text from his father.

Open the door.

He saw the three dots, indicating she was typing.

Why?

I'm outside and it's really cold.

He got out of his car and went to the mudroom door.

Outside where?

His fingers were chilled now as he wondered why even a text conversation with Karina had to be so complicated.

YOUR HOUSE.

The mudroom door opened. "What are you doing here?" she demanded.

"Can I come in?" He shivered in the night chill.

She stepped aside.

"I came to help," he told her.

"You…you…what?"

He looked at her completely confused face. She really had not expected him to come.

She shook her head at him. "Go home. I'm fine."

"Don't be ridiculous. There's a ton of work. And I can help."

She considered him. Clearly, she really wanted the help.

"Listen. This doesn't make us friends or whatever. I just don't want people saying that my sous chef catered a party badly." He shrugged.

"Your sous chef?" She tried to hide her grin, but the amusement shone in her beautiful eyes. "Ha. More like your head chef."

"That would be worse, wouldn't it? If the head chef of Fusion couldn't even cater a party? I'm just looking out for our reputations."

"Fine." She sighed. "Come on in. There's plenty to do since you're such a glutton for punishment."

"Just looking out for the restaurant," Aneel said as he took off his shoes and coat.

"You're a good man," Karina said with a roll of her eyes.

"Thanks. I try." He grinned at her groan of frustration. He hunted down his apron before washing his hands. "What are we working on right now? Because I had an idea for a deconstructed dessert that I believe would be a hit."

"Fine. Let's hear about this dessert." She leaned against the island, her arms folded in front of her. He could have sworn he saw her smile.

"So we can take just about any ladoo, or even a barfi, and deconstruct it down to its parts. How about a faluda?" He raised his eyebrows.

Karina stared at him a moment before she started nodding. Faluda was a milk-and-ice-cream-based dessert with rose, chia seeds and vermicelli noodles. It was usually eaten with a straw and spoon.

"Scoop the ice cream," he started. "Rose-flavored ice cream would work."

Karina shook her head. "Too much rose. We don't want them to be feel like they're eating a whole flower shop. If we use a very good quality vanilla, the rose syrup can do the speaking instead," she said, leaning toward him.

Excitement coursed through him like it always did when he knew he was onto something good. "If we had time, I'd say we make the ice cream ourselves. We would of course soak the chia seeds."

"And the vermicelli." She pointed a finger as her face brightened. "But keep them slightly al dente, you know?" She paused. "Why can't we make the ice cream?"

He raised his eyebrows. "I guess we could. If we start right now."

Karina locked her eyes with his and giggled. "I actually have cream in the fridge. And Param's mom, who lives behind us, has some too."

"Perfect. We could serve it like a sundae." She was standing close enough that he could see the light in her eyes. His heart rate picked up.

"Sprinkled with a few crushed pistachios." She bit her bottom lip in excitement.

"And pink and red sprinkles," he finished.

"I love that idea. So simple. Easier to execute than actual faluda." She was glowing.

"Exactly." A feeling of pride welled inside him, but not because of his dessert idea—more like because he was able to make her glow like that.

"Mrs. Arora will love it." Karina nodded. "Thank you."

"Of course."

Karina had paused to look at him and she was smiling. It was the first time she had looked at him without suspicion or animosity.

He held her gaze.

She stepped back as if only now realizing how close to him she was. "Well, we should get to work. The chicken kabobs aren't going to skewer themselves. And now we're making ice cream."

"We got this," Aneel said, trying to ignore the warm feeling he got when he said *we*.

Chapter Fourteen

The second Monday competition came around, and this time the challenge was Indian street food. Aneel happily applied his fusion ideas while maintaining the same or quite similar flavors to the requested pav bhaji—a potato-based vegetable sloppy joe type deal.

Sonny Pandya, whose restaurant was basically Indian Street food, was completely impressed. He even asked Aneel to go over some of the recipes. Deepak stepped in and told Sonny that until someone was named head chef, recipes could not be shared with competitors.

"Deepak," Aneel explained. "I'm totally okay sharing recipes. It's how we all get better. I don't believe in gatekeeping—"

"Not until after the competition," Deepak said and walked away.

Aneel was declared the winner this week, and Karina smiled and congratulated him, most likely deferring to the fact that street food was a strength for him. Which was true. Street food allowed him to be as creative as he wished.

"Though Deepak was pretty harsh about the sharing recipes thing," Karina said to him. "Sorry, it was hard not to hear."

Aneel shook his head. "Sharing is what makes us better. Helps us be more creative."

A smirk came over her face. "I know. Imagine how good you could be if Sonny Pandya could teach you something."

He scowled at her, and she chuckled as she quickly left the restaurant.

Aneel was in his element the next day as he took charge of the kitchen. He had gone to the market bright and early and done the shopping. He'd half expected Karina to be there and ignored the pang of disappointment that she wasn't. Likely taking advantage of being able to take Veer to school.

It felt good, being at the head of the kitchen, like he belonged there. He delegated assignments that worked to each staff member's strengths as opposed to what their job title was. He had noted, last week, who was good at what.

They were hesitant at first, not comfortable doing what was "supposed to be" someone else's job. Karina stepped up.

"Guys. Chef Rawal comes to Fusion with a great deal of experience. While none of us…" she looked at him "…are thrilled with this competition, we simply have to deal. Chef Rawal is the executive chef this week. He's earned it. You have been given your assignments, and I…" she waved a piece of paper "…have been given mine as well. Let's do this."

"I could have gotten them to work," Aneel mumbled later to Karina.

"Absolutely you could have," she answered.

He studied her face for any sign of sarcasm or taunting and found none. "Then why did you do that?"

"I wanted to help," she said. "Not that you truly needed it. It's just that when big changes are made, if the person they are used to is completely on board, the rest of the team comes on board faster."

Warmth flooded through him, and his smile reflected that. "You had my back."

"Yeah. Whatever. Don't go getting all gushy on me." She walked away, but he saw the smile on her face. "Just looking out for the reputation of the restaurant."

The evening went off without a hitch. Not that everything

went completely smoothly, but whatever came up, he dealt with. The staff had a few rough spots as they adjusted to new roles, but they would get better at it.

Karina was the perfect second. She made sure everyone knew where they should be and what they were doing. The flow of the evening was mainly due to her skills and the faith that the staff had in her. He must have misjudged her when he assumed that she did not appreciate her staff. Loyalty like this was earned, and not without her showing her appreciation.

He would have to earn that loyalty from them.

But honestly, he felt like he was made for this.

"Nicely done tonight," Karina said to him as they both helped the staff clean up, even though they did not have to. The adrenaline was always so high in his body, he needed to do *something*.

"Thank you," he said, his heart warming at her compliment. In the past two and half weeks, he had learned that Karina Mistry rarely gave compliments, but when she did, they were heartfelt.

He was wiping down the counters. "You ran out so fast yesterday, I didn't get to ask. How did the party go?"

"Yeah, I had to get Veer. The party was very successful. Your deconstructed faluda was a huge hit. Thanks for the idea."

"Wait. Are you saying nice things to me?" He held her gaze for a minute. He hadn't noticed before the green flecks in her eyes. Maybe the lighting?

She pursed her mouth. "I might be, Chef Rawal. But don't get used to it."

He smiled. He found that he smiled around her quite a bit. And it felt good. Like he hadn't *really* smiled in a long time. "I could get used to you being nice to me," he said softly.

Something fiery flickered in her eyes as if she were trying to discern his sincerity. They softened, along with the features in her face as she leaned toward him to whisper. "Well, then you would also have to be nice to me."

He moved closer to where she was leaning against the stainless-steel counter, close enough to catch her scent. Citrus. "I don't think I would find that difficult at all." He felt a flush come to his face. Damn, he was like a teenage boy around her. Flustered as if he had never spoken to a beautiful woman before.

To be fair, he had not ever spoken to a woman as beautiful as Karina. Or as intimidating. Or as pleasantly confounding. Unless he counted the younger version of her. But this version was infinitely more interesting and attractive.

He leaned against the counter. She met his gaze.

"Chef Rawal?" Jacob called out to him as he approached, and the moment was gone. Jacob looked from Aneel to Karina. "Sorry to interrupt, but there's someone here to see you."

"Yeah. Okay." Aneel broke his gaze from Karina. "I'll be right out. Probably my sister wanting food." He wiped his hands and made for the dining room, slightly irritated that Saira's visit had interrupted what had been an actual *moment* with Karina. But he froze when he saw who had come to see him.

"Aneel." The deep rumble was like a knife in his back.

Every muscle in his body tensed at the sound of that voice. "When someone doesn't respond to your calls and texts, it means they do not want to communicate with you," Aneel spat.

The man before him was fit and wore an expensive suit. The last time Aneel had seen his father, the day his mother had kicked his father out of the house, he had been a shell of a human. Vacant eyes, almost malnourished looking. He now had a full head of wavy graying hair. His skin glowed with health in the same shade of dark brown as Aneel's, and his eyes were bright and as dark brown as his. Even Aneel knew he was the spitting image of his father.

"I heard that you worked here—"

"How?" Aneel barked. "How could you have possibly heard that?"

Yogesh Rawal clamped his lips together and did not reply. That was answer enough.

Aneel shook his head. "Saira?" Anger flared inside him toward his sister, toward this man, quickly followed by anger at their father for contacting Saira in the first place. His breath came hard as he felt his blood move from a simmer to a boil. "I told her not to talk to you. I told her to block your calls."

"Like you did?" Yogesh Rawal asked softly.

Aneel fired up. "Of course I did. I have nothing to say to you. So I'm not really sure why you came here."

"I want to talk to you. To explain—"

"There is nothing to explain. And I do not care what you want. Mom kicked you out after warning you for years to get help for your addiction." Aneel glared at him, trying to sear him with his eyes.

"That's not the whole story."

"I. Do. Not. Care." Aneel's mother had worked herself to the bone to provide for them, in the end dying from a disease that might have been prevented had she been able to see a doctor. "You can leave. And stop talking to my sister."

"She's my daughter."

"The hell she is. *I* raised her. You leave her be."

"She called me."

Aneel froze. His heart fell into his stomach. How was that possible? She never said anything.

"She knew you would react like this. That's why she didn't tell you." Yogesh Rawal's voice was disturbingly calm. Aneel's memories of his father's voice were that of shouting, crying, begging, slurring. He had squashed those memories away and sealed the lid.

"It doesn't matter. You will discontinue contact with her. And with me."

"I was hoping we could talk. That enough time had passed that—"

"There will never be enough time that would make me want to talk you about anything," Aneel growled. "Never enough time will pass that I would want to forgive you."

"I'm not foolish enough to ask for forgiveness. I only ask that you hear me out." Yogesh Rawal stared at him, something burning in his eyes.

"There is nothing you could say that I would ever want to hear. Leave and do not contact either of us, ever again."

"Your sister is a grown woman."

"My sister has no idea what kind of man you are."

"Were." Sad resignation replaced the burn in Yogesh Rawal's eyes. "I'm sorry."

"Get out," Aneel said with steely calm.

Without another word, his father turned and left. As soon as the door closed, Aneel collapsed into the closest chair.

It was only then that Aneel became aware of the fact that Karina had followed him out and had seen and heard everything.

"So that's your dad, huh?" She should go home. This was none of her business. She had followed him with the intent of getting food for his sister but stopped when she heard his raised voice.

Aneel just nodded. He had slumped the minute the older man left. As if it had taken all of his strength to stand up to him.

"What happened?"

"Now who's curious?" he grumbled.

Karina simply shrugged. His eyes lacked their usual glint. He looked pale and beaten. This was not a version of himself that Aneel often let out. She knew it instinctively. "I showed you mine. You show me yours."

Aneel offered her half a smirk, then inhaled deeply. "He left when I was like ten. My mom finally kicked him out after years of begging him to get help for his drinking. There had been an accident... I never really knew the details. Just that after the accident, he never came back. Saira was maybe three, four. I doubt she remembers him much."

"That's rough."

He shrugged. "We were okay. Mom made enough as a line cook to pay the bills and feed us. But things like saving for college weren't really a priority, you know? Then we lost her..." He trailed off, and the pain in his eyes was too familiar to her.

"He has some nerve coming in here." Aneel stood abruptly. "And what is Saira doing talking to him?" His brown eyes blazed, and he began pacing. "She had no idea what he was like. I'm glad she doesn't remember, but he... Nothing good will come from interactions with him."

Karina watched while he paced and talked, getting increasingly more agitated and angry with every step. "So, hey. It's like 11:00 p.m."

He stopped and looked at her. "So?"

"You said you were good at deconstructing, and your deconstructed dessert was..." she bobbed her head back and forth "...pretty good."

"Yeah?"

"I need something deconstructed." She shrugged. "You could come to the house and check it out."

He stared at her for a few seconds, then heaved a huge sigh and ran a hand through his hair. "Are you asking for my help?" He quirked a smile. "Again?"

"Well, technically, this is the first time because last time I paid you." She stood.

"No. This is the second time."

Her request having the desired effect, she walked to the back and gathered her things.

Aneel followed. He collected his things as well, removing his whites and donning his leather jacket. He simply carried a crossbody bag, while she had a purse, her lunch bag and a backpack. What on earth?

"I'm just not...*proficient* at deconstruction," she insisted as he held the door open for her. As she passed, she caught a whiff of the leather and spice scent she associated with him. She tried not to think about the *something* that had passed between them right before Jacob had interrupted.

Once outside, the night chill cooled her from the heat of the kitchen. September without the sun was chilly. Proper autumn was impending.

"So you admit it, I am better at something than you are." His voice was low, but carried the taunting tone she was coming to know so well.

"I wouldn't go *that* far..."

He chuckled, and it was a relief to see those dimples again. And of course the sight of them made her belly go to mush. He stopped as she opened the door to her car. The smile was gone, and his pain was evident.

"Thanks," he said softly, his eyes suddenly glassy. "For doing this."

Her heart literally ached for what he was going through. "I'm not doing—"

"Karina." His voice shook. "Thank you for the distraction."

She nodded, then forced some lightness into her voice. "Well, let's see if you can even help me with this," she challenged.

His eyes cleared up, and he laughed. "Oh, I can." He waited for her to get in her car and pull out before he walked to his own.

What Karina usually did after a long night like this was

meditate to calm her mind so she could sleep. It was just that the look on his face... She'd been there. Adrenaline coursing through your body, agitation slicing through you—it was near impossible to sleep at these times. She had always found cooking to be a soothing distraction when meditation did not work. She suspected it would help him, too.

A voice in her head that sounded very much like either Sona or Rani asked why she was so eager to give up her own sleep to help him. She told her sisters' voices to shut up and leave her be. She didn't need to investigate all that right now.

Chapter Fifteen

"What are we deconstructing?" His voice was soft and low as he followed her into the house.

Karina dropped her bags in the mudroom with a sigh and met his gaze. He was handsome. She had noticed him instantly that first day of their competition. She was attracted to him after their first conversation, when it became evident that he had no idea how handsome he was and that he was exceedingly kind and happy. She never would have guessed from those interactions all those years ago what kind of pain he'd been through. Even now, not fifteen minutes after a highly charged run-in with his estranged father, he was calmer, already focusing on the task at hand.

"Have a seat." She gestured to the island before turning to retrieve two wineglasses. She poured them each wine and handed him his.

"So this…is made from green grapes." He smirked at her.

She put her hand to her heart and batted her eyelashes. "Why, you are ever so smart," she simpered, then rolled her eyes as they clinked glasses. She took a deep gulp and opened the freezer. "Red wine gives me a headache."

She might as well have been baring her soul to him as she reached into the back of the freezer. Though he had to know what she was getting, after that little scene last week. She stretched her arm behind the ice cream, behind the kulfi, behind the containers of frozen dhal and chicken curry, until she felt the plastic Ziploc bag. She tugged, and it gently came out.

She placed the masala on the island and glanced at Aneel. Her heart thudded against her ribs, and her nose prickled, signaling tears. She inhaled deeply. This was not the time for those tears.

He was sipping his wine and watching her closely. Maybe this wasn't such a good idea.

Too late.

Karina opened the three layers of Ziploc bags until she came to the final plastic bag which held a light brown powder. She looked at Aneel.

"You know what this is." She pressed her lips together. He was watching her with a gentleness in his face that was comforting, his full lips set gently in a small smile that allowed her to go on. "I have tried to figure out the recipe over the years, but I'm always off—just a little bit, you know?" She moved the bag toward him. "So, yes. I am asking you to help me, please."

He held her gaze and took another sip of his wine. He watched her long enough that she thought he might refuse. Then without warning, he smiled and leaned down toward the bag and inhaled.

He lifted his head, his eyes closed as if savoring the aroma of the spices. Long lashes lay against dark skin, and Karina found herself taking advantage of his closed eyes to take in the details of his face. A light scruff had developed on his very defined jaw, his nose was slightly crooked, as if he'd broken it at some point, but it was his mouth that drew her. Full lips forming a small smile drew her gaze, and the loud thudding in her chest simply increased its speed.

He popped open his eyes, and she quickly looked away, raising her wineglass to her lips. A furtive glance at him, and she found him looking at her, as if he knew she'd just been thinking about how his mouth would feel against hers.

"Let's make a cup of chai with it and see how it tastes," he suggested. "But let's not add the milk. I simply want to taste the masala."

She nodded and pulled out their smallest chai pot. Every Indian household had one or two. She made the chai and poured them each a half a cup.

Aneel brought the mug up to his nose and inhaled deeply before tasting.

Karina hesitated before sipping, feeling his eyes on her. She could not remember the last time she'd had this chai masala.

That was a lie. She knew exactly when. It had been a couple months before her mom died. She had been home from college for the weekend.

Karina wrapped her hands around the mug, letting the warmth soak through her palms. She inhaled the aromas of cinnamon, clove and cardamom. "Mom. Seriously, no one makes masala like you do." She sipped and let the flavors entertain her tongue.

"You better believe it. It's my special blend." She sipped at her own chai. "Only I know the secret." She smiled.

"And you're not going to share." Karina rolled her eyes.

"Not today." Her mother laughed.

Karina snapped her head up from the memory. How had she not noticed before that Veer had her mother's laugh?

They had sat right here at this island talking about all the things that mothers and daughters chatted about over chai. For Karina and her mom, it was always spices and food. Karina had asked one more time before leaving for campus for the chai masala secret, as she always did. Her mom had refused, telling her she would have it in good time. Spoken like a person who had no idea that her time was coming to an end.

The next time Karina saw her mother was in a hospital bed, a day before she died.

She closed her eyes and inhaled. The spices hit her nose.

Cinnamon, clove, cardamom, black pepper, nutmeg. And she was having chai with her mom again.

Maybe this wasn't such a good idea. She opened her eyes, well aware that a tear was running down her cheek, to find Aneel watching her.

"We don't have to do this," he said softly.

"No. We do." She wiped her eyes. "It'll never not be like this, but I want to replicate her masala. Though I do remember her saying there was a secret to it." She shook her head. "She never told me."

"You always drink coffee." It was an observation, not of what she did but of what she didn't do. "Your whole family drinks chai—"

"Because I can't stand it." Her voice caught, but she couldn't stop now. "I can't stand drinking chai that my mom didn't make." Tears flowed freely now. "It makes me miss her more."

"Do your sisters know this?"

She shook her head. "I never... I don't tell them this stuff." She looked in his eyes so he would understand—she had never told anyone this.

He nodded, his eyes warm and understanding. "We have an old Formica table. We always sat there while she cooked, and we did homework or talked to her or argued," he said softly. "When we moved into the new place, it came with us. We never talked about it, Saira and I, it's just there. Old, stained, oblivious to its new environment."

She nodded, unable to stop the flow of tears. Aneel just sat with her, watching. Then he set his mug down and turned to her. He slowly moved his hands to her face, as if waiting for her to bat them away. But she did not. He rested his hands on her cheeks, his thumbs wiping away her tears. His hands were rough from work, but there was true comfort there.

When her tears stopped, he lowered his hands. "We really don't have to do this."

"Yes." She sniffled, her voice still thick with tears. "We do."

"Okay." Aneel looked at her apprehensively. "If you're sure."

"I am." And she sounded stronger to herself.

"Because I don't want to be responsible for breaking the big and scary Karina Mistry." He widened his eyes in mock fear.

Who was cheering who up here? She chuckled. "If you aren't *capable* of deconstructing this masala, we can stop."

He gave her a withering look. "Let's look through your spices." He stood, and they pulled out the whole spices that they needed.

Karina wiped her face and blew her nose. She took out her three spice grinders, and they went to work. "I used to help my mom make her chai spice. It was one of the first things we did together."

"But you don't know the secret?"

She shook her head. "I thought I did, because of course I paid attention to the proportions, but when I tried years ago to replicate it, it just wasn't right."

"Maybe you're just too close, you know? Might help to have an outside perspective."

"Which is why you're here," Karina said, allowing a bit of hope into her heart. Maybe all was not lost. Maybe they could make more chai spice, and she'd always have this piece of her mother.

She opened up her laptop where she had logged all previous attempts at this endeavor. He studied her notes with a concentration she had not yet seen from him.

"Okay." He stood from leaning over the computer. "Let's start with roasting and blending each of the spices, then we'll figure out the proportion." He picked up a spoon and held it over the bag. "Just one spoon, I promise. For us to dry taste."

She nodded, and he scooped up one spoon of the masala and put it in a small bowl she had gotten out.

She met his gaze. "Let's taste."

They each stuck a pinky into the mix. Maybe her pinky grazed his. Maybe she liked that small touch as much as she had liked his hands on her face.

They tasted the mix.

"Cinnamon," she said.

"Yes. But the cardamom is stronger. The cloves are there, but in the back."

She nodded and put a pan on the stove, turning the gas to low. Beside her, Aneel tossed on some cinnamon sticks, his arm grazing hers. She shook the pan and let the heat work the spice. When the cinnamon was fragrant, she set it aside. Aneel, still standing beside her, added cardamom to the pan. She heated the pods through, letting them roast a bit. They continued this process with all the spices. Aneel never left her side, and she definitely liked the feel of him standing so close.

They blended and mixed and tasted but could not quite get it. When she had done this on her own, she had spent most of the time frustrated or in tears. With Aneel, it was fun. She couldn't remember the last time she'd enjoyed herself this way. She didn't really have anyone she could talk "food" with. To be fair, she couldn't remember the last time she'd had any fun. She was usually just focused on getting through each day.

"I thought for sure this was the combo," he said, tasting the original as well as the latest mixture.

Karina shrugged. "Yeah...well." Maybe it wasn't meant to be.

Aneel tapped her hand with his finger to get her attention. She looked at him. "The other thing to consider is the age of your mom's masala. It's been in there how many years?"

"Fifteen."

"That may be too long." He looked at her with sad eyes. "Any of these could be the correct combination of the original." He waved his hand over the ten small jars they had made. "But they won't taste the same as our sample, because our sample is old."

She shook her head, gazing at the ten small bottles on the island. She could not—would not accept that. "They taught us deconstruction in culinary school," she said, reaching over for her wine. "And I was the worst at it."

Aneel widened his eyes in horror and put a hand on his chest. "We're starting to get a list of things that Karina Mistry is not good at. Not sure how we'll handle all that."

"Shut up. Deconstruction brought my GPA down." She elbowed him. "How did you learn if you never even went to culinary school?"

"My mom." He looked at her. "Made me deconstruct everything we ever ate. Like even my omelet." He chuckled and looked away as if he were peering into the past.

"We're a pair, aren't we? Missing our moms," she said quietly.

The doorbell rang just then, pulling her out of her thoughts. Aneel glanced in the direction of the front door. Who was ringing the bell at this hour?

Chapter Sixteen

Karina jogged to the door, lest they ring again and wake Veer. She peered out the window. A young man and woman were outside her house.

"It looks like a young couple—"

Aneel came into the foyer. "It's not a couple." He was holding his phone. "My sister has been calling and texting." He opened the door.

"Bhaiya! Seriously, what are you doing here? It's 2:00 a.m.," the young woman said by way of greeting.

"I'm...working. What are you doing here? And you called Tyler?" Aneel nodded at his best friend standing behind his sister.

"Hey." Tyler focused dark blue eyes on him over her head. "She called looking for you. I didn't want her driving alone in the dark." Aneel would have expected no less from him.

"I *am* fine. I could have driven here myself," Saira insisted, giving each of them her you're-lucky-there-is-someone-else-here-look. "I was worried. You're never this late, and you always respond to texts."

"How did you find me?"

"I tracked your phone."

"Please come in. It's gotten really cold. And I don't need my son to wake up," Karina said.

Saira looked at Karina as if just noticing her. Saira's jaw dropped, and she side-eyed Aneel as they followed Karina to the kitchen. Tyler clearly watched the exchange pass between them.

"Hi. I'm Karina Mistry." Karina held out her hand to Saira.

"I know who you are," Saira said, her voice a bit cold. "I'm Saira. This is Tyler." She waved a dismissive hand at him. Her gaze moving between Aneel and Karina.

Aneel raised an eyebrow at his sister.

"Of course." Karina smiled. "You've changed quite a bit in seven years, I didn't recognize you. Sorry."

He pressed his eyes closed and gave a small shake of his head.

It didn't matter. Saira was going to say whatever. "My brother used to talk about you all the time," she said dryly, making it clear what she thought of that.

Karina raised an eyebrow at him, clearly amused. He shook his head as if he had no idea what his sister was talking about.

Karina looked at Saira, a light in her eye. "Of course. You wanted to be a vet."

"How did you know—" Saira started, but Karina cut her off.

"Please," she said, waving a hand. "Your brother talked about you all the time."

"She's in vet school right now." Aneel knew he beamed with pride. But he really was proud of her. And Saira did not seem to be willing to make conversation.

"That must be so exciting," Karina said. "Well, you came all this way, can I get you anything?" she asked, ever the host.

"It's 2:00 a.m.," Saira repeated, her voice like icicles once again.

Karina said nothing, but she nodded, clearly starting to get the picture.

"Thanks, but we're good," Tyler answered, his hands on Saira's shoulders as if he were getting ready to steer her out.

"Let me help clean up before we go," Aneel said. He had

a few things to talk to his sister about, and he did not want to do it with an audience—even Tyler.

Karina waved him off. "It's fine. It'll just take a few minutes."

"He never leaves a mess behind. You might as well let him help," Saira said with a sigh.

So Aneel packed away the spices while Karina loaded the dishwasher and wiped the island down.

"Thank you," she said at last. "I really do appreciate your help tonight."

"Anytime. Happy to come back and try again." If Saira hadn't come, he would have sat in this woman's kitchen all night.

Aneel left behind Saira and Tyler, glancing at the door as it closed behind him. He'd figure out that masala.

"That's Karina Mistry? The scary, competitive Karina Mistry?" Tyler asked as they walked to their cars. Tyler had an inch on Aneel and currently sported a short cut with wavy hair that he liked to run his hands through. He did so now.

"The one and only," Aneel answered.

Tyler shook his head and chuckled.

"What?"

"You're ridiculous. She's gorgeous and smart. You should be dating her," Tyler said.

"No." That was Saira. Both men turned to her. "She's not his type."

"You don't even know her," Aneel said.

"And you do, all of a sudden?" Saira snapped.

"Better than you," Aneel snapped back.

"Are you saying you want to date her?" Saira asked, her eyes narrowing.

"I don't want to date anybody. I wish you would tell that to your auntie friends in the building." But he had enjoyed his time with Karina this evening. He had enjoyed her proximity and her wit. She was relaxed and fun. She had been so vulnerable with him. A warm feeling fell over him, he'd never seen her the way she was tonight. But he certainly wouldn't mind seeing her like this again. Not to mention she had invited him over just to distract him from the visit from his father.

"Okay. Okay. Break up the sibling squabble." Tyler waved his hands at both of them.

"Why? Do you want to date her, Tyler?" Saira threw at Tyler, a challenge in her voice that Aneel was not familiar with.

Tyler's eyes bugged out. "No. Of course not," he blurted. "My friend Aneel clearly has a thing for her."

"No, I don't."

"Dude. It's 2:00 a.m., and you were cooking. In her house," Tyler said, like that sealed everything. "And you showed no signs of leaving, had we not shown up."

"Yeah. You're right. We'll be getting married next week." Aneel shook his head at his friend. "Thanks for not letting Saira come out here alone in the middle of the night. I'll see you later."

"Sure." Tyler nodded at them both as he went to his car.

"I would have been fine," Saira said to Tyler's back. He waved a hand without turning around.

Tyler knew all about their dad. He was there when their mom passed, and his mother cooked for them while they grieved. Anytime life was too much, Aneel and Saira knew they had a spot in the Hart household. So it was not unusual for Saira to reach out to Tyler and his family if she was worried about Aneel.

"Come on, Saira. Let's go home." Aneel got into his car, and Saira followed suit.

"What the hell were you doing here?" she said without preamble.

"What the hell are you doing calling Yogesh Rawal?" he shot back as he pulled away from the curb.

Silence floated between them.

"I'm sorry I didn't answer my phone. I was helping Karina with something," Aneel said after a few minutes of driving.

"I was worried." True concern colored her words. "You're all I have."

"I know." He softened. "I'll remember to text if I'm going to be extra late." He waited a beat. "Yogesh Rawal came to see me today. At work."

Saira tensed in the seat beside him. "Fine. Yes. I called him." She lifted her chin and turned to him. Defiant. She looked just like their mother.

"Why would you do that?" Aneel fought to keep his voice level. What he really wanted to do was shout at the top of his lungs.

"Because, Bhaiya, he's our dad."

"He was never our dad."

"Whatever, Bhaiya. Look, he reached out a couple years ago, and I never responded."

"You didn't tell me—" Aneel started, firing up.

"Yeah, because I knew you would do this." She waved her hand over him, indicating his aggressive posture. "Anyway, a couple months ago, I responded to a text of his from a year before."

"Why?"

"Because he kept saying he had changed, and he missed us."

"Bullshit. He wants something."

"No, Bhaiya, he doesn't—"

"You're too naive, Saira. You don't remember. You don't know what he was like." Images flooded his mind for the second time that night of his parents screaming at each other, their mother crying, his father passed out on the bathroom floor.

"I remember a little." Her voice was small.

"Then why would you want to talk to him?"

"Because he's our dad," she said again. "He's our family."

"I thought we were each other's family."

"We are. This doesn't change that. You don't have to talk to him if you don't want. But I want to."

"No."

She raised her eyebrows. "No?"

"No."

"That's not even a thing. You cannot tell me no."

"I'm telling you that I do not want you in contact with that man. I do not care what stories he's spinning. Mom kicked him out for a reason."

"What reason?"

"That he was an alcoholic."

"Maybe Mom was wrong," she said to him.

He stared at his sister, then back at the road, then his sister again. This young woman he had watched over since she was born. He used to have her watch TV in his room, the volume blaring so she couldn't hear their father swearing at their mother. When their father left, he became her father figure, and when their mom died, he became her mother, too. Everything he did, *everything* was for her.

But in that moment, when she questioned if their mother was right in kicking out their father, when she was *insisting* she see their father, he had no idea who she was. The thought flitted across his brain…maybe he never had known.

"Mom was not wrong," he seethed at her. "You can't see him." He parked the car in front of their building, and they got out.

She was quiet on the way up to the apartment. Maybe he had gotten through.

As soon as they entered, she turned to him, eyes fierce, back straight. "I am a grown adult, and I can see who I want. I can give our dad a second chance if he asks for it. You…" she poked his chest "…cannot stop me." She paused for breath.

"You have to stop telling me what to do. I'm not a little girl anymore. As soon as I can find a place, I'm moving out."

"Saira—"

She held up a hand. "You know, I was going to ask what you were doing at Karina Mistry's house at 2:00 a.m., but…" she shook her head "…I don't care. You want to set yourself up for destruction, you go ahead. It's not my problem." She turned on her heel and went to her room.

Chapter Seventeen

Karina was groggy the next morning and opted for an extra shot of espresso in her coffee. She did not want to consider the possibility that she might not be able to replicate her mother's chai masala. That she would lose her mother all over again.

She had, however, enjoyed the challenge. The camaraderie of a colleague to bounce ideas off of. Her enjoyment had nothing to do with how he had looked at her, his eyes soft with compassion or sparkling with amusement. It had nothing to do with how it had felt to stand close to him. She should regret her moment of vulnerability, but she did not. She knew enough about Aneel, and how he'd behaved in that moment, to know that he did not think less of her. He made her feel safe, in a way she hadn't felt since she lost her mother. That last cup of chai with her was the last time she had felt truly herself.

"Mommy." Veer's sleepy voice drifted to her from the steps. She went and picked him up. "I need to defrost."

"Me, too." She carried him to the sofa and laid his head on her lap while checking her emails on her phone. Another one from Chirag. Her thumb hovered over it as she looked at her son. He was peaceful with the family he had. He did not need the complications of his bio-father returning and whatever that entailed. Look at how Aneel's father's return was tearing him apart—a grown man. She deleted the email without reading it.

At least Aneel was head chef this week. It gave her a chance to breathe after that party and running the restaurant last week. All she had to do was show up and follow his direction.

A couple emails popped up from someone she didn't know. Subject line—Catering. It was from a woman, Payal Patel requesting her catering services for a small law office one-year-anniversary-celebration.

Payal then gave a dollar amount she was willing to pay, and Karina nearly dropped the phone. That was a ton of money for an office party.

She responded back that she would be happy to cater the event, and two weeks from Monday evening worked best. It was the one day she wasn't working in the restaurant, and she would have two weeks to prep. She was suddenly quite wide awake, her brain almost in overdrive as she came up with menu ideas.

She sent some of her ideas to Payal to get a feel for what she wanted. Payal was prompt in her replies, and within an hour, Karina had a working menu and a fifty percent deposit Venmo'd to her.

The second was from a well-known wedding planner in the area, who also happened to be Param's ex-fiancée, Sangeeta Parikh. Her thumb hovered over it. Whatever, Param was with Rani now. She tapped it open.

Dear Karina,

Sangeeta Parikh here. I know it's awkward to hear from me because of my history with Param. I heard he married Rani, and I am super happy for them both. I'm currently seeing Sonny Pandya, and he told me what a fabulous chef you are and, more to the point, that you also cater. I have a client who is getting married in a month, but their caterer canceled. I realize that this is very last minute, but is there any way you can pull off a wedding with 500 guests in about a month? It's a second wedding for them both, so while the guest list is large, they are opting to only have the wedding ceremony and a reception. The bride and groom are willing to make it worth your while.

Please let me know at your earliest convenience.

Best,

Sangeeta Parikh

Karina stared at her phone for a minute, trying to process what was happening. Ideas bombarded her mind, each one better than the last. What to make. How to present it. What went with it. She grabbed her laptop next to her and began to type. She didn't stop until Veer sat up.

Two parties. Two quite *lucrative* parties.

She responded to Sangeeta that the past was in the past, and she would love to help. Sangeeta's reply was immediate and included the name and number of the bride. They could meet whenever it worked for Karina. Karina set up a time for the next morning—she could do it after she dropped Veer off at school.

"Mom. I'm defrosted."

She glanced at the time. Wow. She had lost track, and now Veer might be late. She closed her laptop and stood. Picking up her son, she swung him around. She should be irritated that Aneel had won this past Monday and that he ruled the kitchen this week and would make her add French fries and Tater Tots to classic Indian dishes, but she wasn't.

What she was, was excited about these two events.

"Honestly, it's as if you've never diced onions before," Aneel snapped at the line cooks. "It's imperative that the vegetables be diced perfectly, for the aesthetic."

The kitchen was silent as Aneel grumbled at them. In the almost three weeks he had been in this restaurant, he had never done this, and they were in a bit of shock.

If Karina had said exactly that, they would have barely noticed. She wasn't sure that was necessarily good, but she knew it was not how Aneel usually treated the staff. She had expected that he would be tired after their late night yesterday, but she hadn't thought for a minute that he would be snippy with the staff.

The cameraman floated around the kitchen, catching everything. Aneel glanced at the camera pointed at him and turned to leave the kitchen. "Redo them," he growled.

Karina waited a beat to see if he would return. He did not. He must need a minute. "Okay. You heard him. Let's get this done. Redo the veggies."

The staff moved, locating more vegetables and dicing them as asked.

Karina moved to where the meat was being prepped. She instructed them based on what the menu required, as well as what she thought Aneel would want. Ten minutes passed, and the kitchen was once again active and noisy with the sounds of meals being prepped. Karina walked around, giving instruction and guidance, making sure everything was up to standard.

When Aneel did not return after fifteen minutes, she gave the order to start cooking. Aneel should be here for this, but she had no idea where he was. If they didn't start now, they'd run late all night.

"What the hell are you doing?" Aneel grumbled at Karina as he reentered the kitchen twenty minutes after he left. The prep had been well underway when he left, but the cooking had clearly started without him.

"Just getting the night started," Karina said. She sounded—cheerful. Weird.

"Just taking over my kitchen, in other words," he groused at her. Irritation and anger had eaten at him all night, and it was finally getting an outlet.

"No. I was just making sure—"

"That you were seen on camera running the kitchen during my week. That you were seen being in charge."

Her eyebrows shot up with the volume of his voice. "You stepped out of the kitchen and did not return."

"I was coming back."

"If we didn't get started, we would have been late all night." Karina's eyes flashed at him, but he did not care. She was trying to steal this job from him. Most likely because she still believed that he sabotaged her all those years ago.

He was tired of it. He was tired of paying for mistakes he didn't even make.

"I was trying to help you," she said to him under her breath.

"Ha. I'm supposed to believe that cutthroat Karina Mistry would help her competition?"

She narrowed her eyes at him. "You're right." She started untying her apron. "There's no reason for me to be here." She removed her apron as she made for the door. "I guess I have the night off."

Aneel watched her go. Whatever. She could do whatever she wanted. Just like his sister. Just like his dad.

Karina stomped as far as the office before realization hit her. Something had to have happened to Aneel. The man she had just seen was not the man she'd been hanging out with these past few weeks. Nor was he the man she'd known seven years ago.

"You need to get back in there." Deepak and Rakesh met her in the hallway.

"No. I don't," she snapped back at them.

"The viewers are going to love the drama," Rakesh said. "We have a small sample of people watching, and they just got really excited. Get back in there and fight with him."

Karina looked at Deepak. "Are you crazy? Something

awful must have happened. Or have you not noticed the uber-happy puppy that is the real Aneel Rawal didn't show up to work today?"

Deepak shrugged. "I don't care why he's in a mood. If Rakesh says the sample viewers are loving the tension between you two, then it's really going to show well when we edit. I need you to go back in there and pick a fight."

"I will do no such thing." She folded her arms across her chest. She was not about to go in there and make Aneel look bad because he was having a rough day and it looked entertaining to the viewers. No matter what he might have accused her of.

Deepak smirked at her. "You will if you want a chance at this job. Or any job in any restaurant in this city."

"Excuse me?"

"You were never a fan of his anyway. Just go in there and continue the argument." Deepak stood in front of her. "Or leave. But I promise if you do, you'll never be head chef here. Not to mention I have creative control over this show and I can portray you as difficult to work with. How far will that get you in a new job hunt?"

She stared at him. She had no choice. She was going to have to go in there and pick a fight with Aneel when he was clearly hurting. "Fine," she said, putting on her apron and heading back to the kitchen.

Deepak had not said *what* the fight had to be about.

Karina walked back into the kitchen, retying her apron. "Chef Rawal," she called out, putting some aggression in her voice.

"Yes." He turned to her and already she saw regret and apology in his eyes. Too bad.

"Hands down, the Hulk is the best Avenger." She raised an eyebrow and slightly dipped her chin, willing him to get it.

"Chef Mistry." He pursed his lips. "You are profoundly

mistaken. Hands down, Iron Man is the best Avenger. For many reasons, in fact." He paused to call out orders to the line cook and check everyone's progress. Then he turned to Karina. "These are the reasons, in no particular order." He continued walking around the kitchen, monitoring everything as he spoke.

"One." He raised an index finger over his head as he walked. "He's a scientist who made a robot suit while being held captive. Two." He raised another finger and leaned over a line cook to check progress. He nodded and gave the line cook a smile. "He literally beat up the Hulk using the Hulk-buster suit. Three." He raised a third finger. "He can call the suit to him from almost anywhere. And let's not forget he's a billionaire who funds the Avengers himself."

Karina walked the kitchen as well and helped out while she gave her rebuttal. "I disagree. One." She raised her index finger as Aneel had. "Banner is also a highly intelligent scientist. Two. His strength and size are unmatched. Three. He's basically bulletproof. And let's not forget that he found a way to merge his two identities and get the best of both worlds."

Aneel shook his head at her. "No. That was just weird." But he gave her the first real smile she had seen all day.

Her heart did a flip. That was unexpected. "It was his acceptance of himself," Karina countered.

"You're both wrong," Jacob spoke up. He looked up from where he was frying French fries. "Thor is an actual god."

Karina laughed and many heads turned her way, looks of surprise on their faces. Had she never laughed in this kitchen? The cameras continued to roll.

"All three of you forget who had the greatest power," Rita piped up from the prep counter. "The power of persuasion. Black Widow."

The discussion continued throughout the night as they chopped and cooked and plated. Aneel's shoulders relaxed, and his smile and easy manner returned. Though every so often, Karina would glance at him and catch a look of pain in his eyes she didn't understand.

Aneel had no idea why they were debating the various merits of the Avengers, but he had gleaned enough from the look on Karina's face to go along with it. He had caught the camera focused on him during his blowup and knew the "debate" had something to do with it.

The night ended much better than it had started. There'd been great reception from the diners about his food, which was encouraging, but he still had an ache in his heart and a dark cloud over his head from arguing with Saira. A text from Tyler had told him that Saira was safe at his place.

Aneel lingered at the restaurant, cleaning and recleaning with the staff, dreading the return to the empty apartment. When he finally did return, the apartment was darker and emptier than it had ever been. The silence was deafening, and he was too filled with adrenaline to sleep. Not to mention, he had behaved badly tonight. He grabbed a few spices and got in his car before he thought too much about it.

Ten minutes later, he was parked in front of Karina's house. Thankfully, the kitchen light was still on.

He went to the mudroom door and knocked lightly. In minutes, the door opened, and Karina stood before him, one hand on the curve of her hip, her lips pursed to hide a smile. "Hey." She looked completely unsurprised to see him. Maybe even happy.

"Hey. So, I think the masala is missing the black peppercorns from the Indian store. They have more bite." He spoke as if they were simply continuing a conversation already in progress.

She folded her arms. "You came here after midnight to tell me that?"

He held the jar of peppercorns out to her. "And to give you some." He met her gaze. "As a peace offering and apology, along with my deepest gratitude."

She inhaled, but she gave a small smile and stepped aside to let him in. "Honestly, Iron Man is the hill you're going to die on?"

"The Hulk. Are you serious?" The faint aroma of citrus still clung to her, ever after a whole day in the kitchen. He handed her the jar as he brushed past her.

They entered the kitchen, and he turned to take her in as she walked toward him. Messy bun, leggings, no makeup. His heart thudded in his chest. She was wearing an oversize… "Hulk T-shirt?" He sank into those hazel eyes.

"Deepak and Rakesh insisted I continue arguing with you. Apparently, the sampling of live viewers responded well and immediately to the tension between us. Both Deepak and Rakesh insisted that the tension between us was great for the show. If I didn't turn back around and pick a fight with you, I was toast." She grinned. "He didn't specify what type of argument."

He nodded. "I am sorry."

"That you think Iron Man is the best Avenger? Apology accepted." She smirked.

"I am sorry I lost it on you, the staff. That was out of line, not only unprofessional but completely disrespectful, not to mention unkind—"

She held up a hand. "I completely agree. That's not the Aneel Rawal we have all come to know. Tell me what happened." She motioned to the island, and he sat. She grabbed two wineglasses and opened a bottle of wine.

He took a gulp of his wine and studied the glass. Karina simply sat next to him and waited. "My dad is an alcoholic.

I have memories of him passed out on the bathroom floor, the kitchen floor, the sofa. I remember my mother threatening him if he wouldn't get help." He looked at Karina before continuing. "There was an accident—I never knew the details—Tyler and his mom came over. My mom was furious." He shook his head. " All I really know is that Mom didn't let him come home after that. Mom simply said he had gone away. I remember that there was a sense of peace in the house that had not existed when he was there, drunk all the time. She never told me what had happened. And I never asked. I didn't care. The cloud of tension had left the house. We were finally happy."

Karina laid her hand on his, and her warmth seemed to travel from his hand throughout his body. She didn't say a word, but her touch said everything to him.

"Anyway. He reached out when Mom died, and I told him to leave us alone. But he's been texting recently, and it turns out it's because Saira contacted him. She told me last night that she's been meeting with him." Aneel's heart tightened at the thought of his father breaking her heart. "I had a huge argument with her about it, and she wants to move out."

Karina squeezed his hand, as if she were trying to infuse strength into him.

"It's not like we were going to live together forever, I know that. I just didn't think she would move out...like this." His voice grew thick with emotion.

"The apartment was pretty empty tonight, huh?" Karina finally said.

He nodded.

"Where is she?"

"She's...uh... Tyler texted me. She's at his place. So she's safe."

"Are you going to talk to her?"

He shrugged. "I haven't changed my mind. I still don't think she should see our dad, and she still wants to."

Something flitted through Karina's eyes, like she went somewhere but came back. She stood. "Let's give the peppercorns a try, shall we?"

Chapter Eighteen

The peppercorns, while a welcome, spicy addition to the masala mix, were not the solution. By the time Aneel left, it was late—again—and Karina was out as soon as her head hit the pillow.

She enjoyed an extra half hour of sleep in the morning, courtesy of not being head chef and needing to constantly check on the restaurant. She took her coffee to the sofa to enjoy defrosting time with Veer, checked her email and found that Payal had asked for a change in the menu. Not a problem. There were two more emails requesting her catering services for small events over the next two weeks. Karina said yes to both. A third email confirmed her meeting with Rajni, Sangeeta's bride.

In a month, she had hoped to have the head chef position at Fusion. She couldn't be catering if she was a full-time head chef. She would do that wedding and that would be it. Thankfully, no more emails from Chirag. Hopefully he had gotten the message and had decided to back off.

She dropped off Veer at school and did some shopping at the farmers market for the events she now had lined up for the next two weeks. She did not scan all the tall dark-haired men at the market looking for Aneel.

No sooner did she step into the restaurant than Deepak and Rakesh called her into the office. Aneel was already there.

He rolled his eyes in her direction before shaking his head at Rakesh and Deepak.

"Listen. The chemistry between you two is off the charts," Rakesh started right in. "My experience tells me that when we air, the viewers are going to love, love the contentious interactions between you two. The small sample of live viewers we have is way more invested in your banter. Even that ridiculous Avengers argument you had last night." He looked at them expectantly.

Karina narrowed her eyes. "So?" She knew what they were getting at, but she needed them to actually say it.

"So," Deepak started, looking at her as if she were the crazy one here, "we need you both to keep arguing."

Silence filled the space.

"You want us to keep fighting with each other, because you think the viewers will enjoy watching us argue?" Aneel sounded incredulous.

"Yes!" Rakesh said. "I don't care if you're really angry or not. Fake it."

"You want us to fake-hate each other?" Aneel stared at them.

Rakesh's smile was huge as he sighed, relieved that they seemed to understand. "Exactly. You are competing for the same job. It makes sense."

"That's ridiculous," Aneel said.

"That's the dumbest thing I have ever heard," Karina said at the same time.

Deepak looked from one to the other. "It doesn't matter what you think. Just make it happen." He and Rakesh left the office, their point made.

Karina looked at Aneel, and they both started laughing. "What the...?" he said.

She shrugged. "I don't know."

Aneel sighed. "What should we fight over today?"

"Let's just wing it. I'm sure you'll irritate me in some way."
She smirked at him.

"So I should just be my normal self?" He raised his eyebrows at her.

"There is nothing more irritating." She chuckled.

Aneel inhaled. "Okay. Let's do this." He grabbed his whites
off the hanger, and she went to get hers.

She sneaked a peek at him while he was fitting his arms
into the sleeves of his whites. He had on a simple fitted black
T-shirt that did nothing to hide the movement of his muscles
as he wiggled into his whites.

Karina slipped hers on as she chuckled at him. "You're
no better than Veer when I make him put on any kind of second layer."

He was buttoning the jacket and squirming as he did it.
"What do you mean?" He lifted his chin to get the buttons
at the neck.

She could not help herself. One step and she was in front
of him, batting away his hands. "Let me."

His sigh was deep and telling.

She laughed again. "Between you and Veer, I'm beginning
to understand males better." She got the buttons and smoothed
out the jacket. Maybe her hands lingered over his chest and
arms a bit longer than necessary.

"Glad to help." His voice was just above a whisper, and she
felt his brown eyes on her.

She swallowed and stepped back. "Ready to fight?"

They entered the kitchen and got to work. Aneel greeted
each member of the staff and joked with them as if they were
all close friends.

"Hey Chef Rawal," Karina called, allowing irritation to
lace her voice. "Are you the mayor of this kitchen or the chef?
Maybe socialize less and work more." She caught Jacob's horrified expression and winked at him, letting him in on the

secret. Just as he had picked up on the Avengers' argument, Jacob immediately seemed to understand what was going on.

"Just because you choose to be the ice queen..."

She snapped her head to him, eyes narrowed, and they were off. They maintained a steady stream of insults and arguments for the couple hours that the camera was on. When the cameras were finally packed away, Karina sagged in relief and saw Aneel's broad shoulders do the same.

Rakesh peeked into the kitchen. "Perfect, you two. Keep it up."

"Sorry." Aneel came up beside her. "Ice queen was too harsh."

She shook her head. "I've been called worse. And I know you were simply playing the role."

He squinted at her, amusement all over his face. "Was I?"

She lightly smacked his arm, coming up against some very hard muscle. "Maybe not any more than I was when I said your Tater Tot chaat was colonized potato trash."

He placed his hand over his heart in mock distress. "You meant that?"

"Truthfully, Tater Tot chaat sounds ridiculous to me. But the customers loved it, so... go you," Karina said. "Though I only insulted your food."

Aneel's face went from amused to horrified in an instant. "You are absolutely right." His hand went to his heart and he cringed. "I'm sorry... I wish I could take it back. It's such a 'guy' thing to say to a woman who threatens his power." He looked horrified. "I was really thinking more Elsa than any-thing—"

She held her hand up. "I accept."

Silence floated between them during which Aneel simply held her gaze. A genuine smile came across his face. "You liked my Tater Tot Chaat, didn't you?" It was an accusation. "Admit it."

"I admit liking Tater Tots. But everybody likes Tater Tots." Karina waved a hand at him and went back to work. No way would she admit to liking something called Tater Tot chaat. "Though I do envy the way you're so friendly and laid-back with the staff."

"It makes it more fun to be in the kitchen all day if you're friendly with the people you spend time with."

She nodded. "I can see that. I've just always maintained that distance so I get their best work. Stick to the rules, you know?"

"The two don't have to be mutually exclusive."

"Well." She grinned. "I'm more likely to get on board with that than I am Tater Tot chaat."

Chapter Nineteen

Aneel did not waste time hanging out alone in his apartment. He went in, grabbed another spice and headed straight to Karina's house. He was greeted by her sister, who did not appear surprised to see him.

"Hey, handsome. How's it going?" Sona winked at him.

"I'm good, Sona," he answered blandly. She seemed to always flirt with him a bit when he would first arrive, then she would stop. He was absolutely not interested. To be fair, she didn't seem interested, either.

Sachin Uncle was nursing a glass of wine at the island when Aneel entered, Sona behind him. Wine was clearly already flowing, despite the hour, and Sachin Uncle and Karina were discussing a menu. Aneel caught sight of the spice grinder which gave him pause and excited him at the same time. She had expected him.

"Hey, Sunshine," Karina called to him from next to her father. She poured wine into an empty glass. "What do you have for me tonight?"

"A different kind of cinnamon."

Karina nodded, took the small jar from him and handed him the glass of wine that she had just poured. He could not remember the last time someone had anticipated any of his needs. She held his gaze a moment and stepped a bit closer under the guise of clinking glasses with him.

"Heard from baby sis?" she asked quietly.

He gave a small shake of his head and turned to Uncle as he sipped his wine. "What's the menu you're all discussing?"

"Karina has another catering job a week from Monday," he answered. "And a couple smaller jobs as well."

"Oh yeah? Who?"

"A small law business. I've been emailing with the office manager, Payal Patel. Coming up on a year and her boss wants to treat the staff to a nice party," Karina offered as she reached for the spice grinder. "The others just want fresh samosas for a party or those pani puri shooters we did for Mrs. Arora. Paratha, that kind of thing."

"What are we making for the small business?" He did not miss the glances that passed between Uncle and Sona.

"Some basic apps, then she wanted traditional food, naan, dhal, a couple shaks." Karina shrugged. "A couple of sweets."

"Let me know what you need me to do," he said, sipping his wine.

She looked at him. "I can handle it."

"I'm happy to help." He paused and made eye contact with her. "It'll keep me...busy."

He saw the understanding in her eyes immediately, and the fight for independence was replaced by compassion. "That would be great. She's paying me a ridiculous amount of money. I could also use help day-of if that works. It's after the competition."

"Of course."

She used the grinder on the cinnamon he brought, and they mixed it up with the other spices. Still not quite there.

"There are other places to get these spices from," Aneel noted. "Though I doubt your mom went to these lengths for her ingredients."

"Oh no, she took her chai masala very seriously," Uncle

said. "She ordered the spices online from all over the world and kept it all a secret for sure."

Karina frowned. "I didn't know that."

"Exactly." Her father grinned. "Even I don't know where she ordered from. Her chai masala was always a project she kept close to her heart." His eyes saddened but lit up in the next second. "I think it kept her connected to her childhood, to her mother." He dropped his gaze on Karina. "Very much like you."

"Then maybe we are in the right direction," Aneel said.

Uncle leaned toward him. "Karina did tell you that her mother was raised in Uganda. Not India."

Karina gasped, and her eyes widened. "I did not tell him. Her family immigrated to Uganda before she was born. She lived there until she left to attend college in India."

Aneel grinned. "So let's try a different path."

Another round was poured, and Aneel sat with Karina's family, enjoying the ribbing and love that filled the kitchen. Sona shared stories from her photo shoots, and he didn't remember the last time he had laughed so hard. They must have been quite loud, as Veer shuffled into the kitchen, rubbing his eyes.

"Mommy. What's so funny?"

Karina gasped at his presence and picked him up. "Just a funny story from Sona Masi," she said, as he curled into her.

Aneel was sitting next to Karina, and without thought, he gently placed a hand on Veer's back. He felt the boy sink into the touch.

"How come you're here so late, Aneel Uncle?"

Sona and Uncle were discussing Sona's business, so Aneel leaned in and said to Veer, "My sister and I were arguing, so I came here for a while."

Veer simply looked at him with those dark, sleepy eyes. "Maybe you just agree to disagree. Then you won't fight."

Aneel chuckled at Veer. "You know..." he glanced at Karina watching him over Veer's head "...that's a great idea." He glanced at the time. "And I should go."

"Here," Sona said, standing up, her arms extended to Karina. "Come to Masi."

Veer transferred himself to his aunt, and Sona and Uncle excused themselves to go to bed.

Karina walked Aneel to the door. "You going to be okay in that lonely apartment?"

He shrugged. "I try not to think about it."

"I got a really big catering offer," she told him quietly, clearly not wanting her family to hear.

"That's fabulous." Happiness filled him. She was killing it. "For when?"

"For after the competition." She studied him. "A wedding. Five hundred people." She leaned close to whisper, "Sonny Pandya's girlfriend is the planner."

Aneel was impressed. "And what did you say?"

"I said yes. The money is awesome."

"Why are you whispering?" he asked.

She set her mouth. "Sonny Pandya's girlfriend, the planner? She was engaged to Param."

His jaw dropped, and he laughed. "The drama."

She widened her eyes. "I know, right?"

"Are you sure you still want to be head chef?" he asked.

"Trying to get rid of the competition, are you?" She smirked at him.

"Hell yes. Going up against you is harder than I thought it would be," Aneel said softly.

Her gaze snapped to his.

Karina Mistry was a talented chef. She could have any position, anywhere she wanted. "I was joking," she said.

He dropped his gaze to her mouth and was visited by the need to feel those lips against his. He lifted his gaze back to her eyes. "I was not."

Chapter Twenty

A light knock at the mudroom door Sunday night put a smile on Karina's face. Fusion closed early on Sunday evening. She had left right after service so she could get Veer ready for the school week and in bed on time. The knock was Aneel coming over, as he had done every night this week.

"Look at her, Param," Sona said loud enough for Karina to hear from the sofa. "That little knock, and our big sister is flushed."

"Have we vetted this guy?" Param asked, ever the protective brother-in-law, forget that Karina was five years his senior.

Karina shook her head. "No need to vet anyone. We're just colleagues. He's helping me duplicate Mom's chai masala. That's all."

"He's not helping with all the catering?" Sona asked, accusation in her voice.

"Well, yes," Karina admitted grudgingly. "But I'm sharing the payment with him for that. Like colleagues do."

"Colleagues." Sona rolled her eyes. "Is that what they call being all googly-eyed?"

"I am not, nor have I ever been googly-eyed over a guy. Besides, I don't really date. I have Veer."

Her brother-in-law and her sister shared a look. "You know that you do not have to remain single just because you have Veer," Sona said, a note of seriousness in her voice.

"I know that." Kind of. "It's just…complicated."

"It's always going to be complicated, Karina." Sona made eye contact. "Sometimes love and happiness are complicated."

"This is just not a good time," Karina insisted.

Param shook his head. "It's never a good time. Doesn't mean it's not going to happen."

Okay, so maybe her heart rate did increase as she neared the door. And maybe she was a bit excited to have Aneel come over every night. The reality was that he was there because he could not stand to be alone in his apartment. And she did have Veer to consider. She wasn't planning on never being in a relationship, but right now was not the time.

"Hey." She opened the door, trying to squash her enthusiasm at seeing him. She might have failed. He was in his leather jacket and jeans, which might be her favorite outfit on him.

Aneel's face lit up, and he handed her a small jar of nutmeg as he walked in, bringing the scent of burning leaves with him. "Wow. That smells amazing. Samosa filling?"

She nodded as she led the way into the kitchen, sliding his glass of wine toward him. "Sona and Param are here to help me fill them."

Aneel removed his jacket as he accepted the wine.

"Hi, Aneel." Sona stood and walked over. "Soo good to see you," she practically simpered as she grazed his arm with her hand.

Karina stiffened at her sister's blatant flirting, as if she hadn't just accused Karina of being googly-eyed. Karina glared at her, and Sona smiled in victory. Karina pressed her lips together. She'd fallen for the oldest sister trick there was. Fine. She rolled her eyes at Sona. *Maybe* she liked him.

Param and Aneel were already in conversation, so hopefully they didn't notice the silent communication between Karina and Sona.

"Free labor," Param was saying as he shook Aneel's hand. "How's it going?"

Aneel grinned, clearly comfortable in everyone's presence. "Great. Let's knock out these samosas." He side-eyed Karina, and her heart flipped at the accompanying smile. "Seeing as how she just *happens* to have the filling ready to go as soon as I get here."

Karina tried and failed to hide her smirk. "Damn straight," she said as she turned to get out equipment. "Everyone in my life works." She brought the deep fry pan to the stove to find Aneel staring at her. A small smile was on his face, his eyes lit up like he'd just won a million dollars.

She realized what she had just said. And she'd meant it. The words had come out without her even thinking about them, but that was because they came from her heart. "Don't get all excited about being in my life," she joked to hide her flush. "It can be a tough place to be."

Aneel did not miss a beat. "I can take it."

It was Karina's turn to be speechless as she felt something snap into place between her and Aneel. She ignored Sona and Param elbowing each other like teenagers behind Aneel.

Param cleared his throat in the thick silence. "I'm teaching a bunch of scary seventh graders in the morning, so I have about an hour before I have to go."

"Right." Karina turned to her brother-in-law, ignoring the knowing look in his eye.

Karina was a stickler for making everything from scratch. That meant no shortcut for the crust. She had made the dough herself, and it was ready to go. She and Aneel began rolling the flat breads, while Param and Sona expertly wrapped the samosas in them.

Karina turned on some music while they worked and talked and laughed.

"You're all really good at the samosa thing," Aneel commented as he continued to roll out flat bread beside Karina. They weren't standing too close, but she was aware of his presence and the comfort she found there as if it were a solid thing between them.

"Our mom was a stickler," Sona said. "Remember?"

Karina nodded, a laugh on her lips. "Every hole had to be closed *super* tight. Mom did not tolerate a drop of oil inside her samosas. If she found a hole, she made you undo it and redo the whole samosa. It was tedious."

Aneel glanced at her. "Our moms would have gotten along so well. My mom's attention to detail in her cooking and everything she did used to drive me nuts. But now I find myself doing those exact same things."

"Not me. I'm way more relaxed about cooking than she was." Karina chuckled as Param and Sona stared at her.

"She's not, is she?" Aneel asked.

"Not even a little bit." Sona shook her head. "I didn't even know she knew the word *relax*."

Karina laughed and left the rolling to Aneel in order to turn on the oil. She would partially fry them today, so the process would be quicker day-of. She picked up the samosas that had been stuffed and inspected them. "No holes. Nicely done, guys."

Param and Sona rolled their eyes.

They continued chatting while Param and Sona stuffed and Karina par-fried the samosas. Forty-five minutes in, Param begged off, citing work the next day. Sona gave a long, exaggerated yawn and also begged off, not so subtly leaving Karina and Aneel alone.

She felt rather than saw Aneel glance at her as her sister went up to bed.

"Well," she said, still not looking at him, because looking at him would make her flush and she didn't want to do that. "It looks like I get to see how well you can stuff a samosa."

Aneel chuckled, a deep, warm sound that vibrated through her body. "Time me."

She snapped her gaze to him. "Are you serious?"

"Let's make it a game. Five minutes, who can successfully stuff the most."

She nearly laughed at him. She used to have these contests with Sona all the time. "You're on."

They set a timer and made samosas as fast as they could. The competition did not keep Aneel from chattering. She was focused on the task at hand, but she was completely aware of his movements beside her.

"My mom and I used to do this," he told her. "I think she just wanted the tedious part done as fast as possible."

"Sona and I used to compete like this, too." She paused and glanced at him. "I always won."

The timer buzzed. Karina did a quick count and turned to face him. "I told you. I always win." She smirked at him.

Aneel stood inches from her, his eyes meeting hers with nothing less than admiration in his eyes. "I have no doubt."

Monday morning rolled around faster than necessary after a late night with the samosas, bringing Karina and Aneel to the third competition. Karina stifled a yawn as she and a tired-looking Aneel waited for Rakesh to announce what the competition would be.

"This week, we'll do a little pivot and have our chefs make some desserts." Rakesh smiled into the camera. No surprise. All he had to say now, was that one of the desserts was—

"Kulfi and gulab jamun."

Perfect. She knew Aneel was smirking without even looking at him. She let out a small chuckle. Deepak and Rakesh had already reminded them about the arguing they wanted. She inhaled and glanced at Aneel.

Let the games begin.

"What everyone doesn't know is that Chef Mistry and I have competed once before," Aneel started.

She rolled her eyes and grimaced at him for the camera. The more she had gotten to know Aneel these past few weeks, the less she found that she cared about something that happened seven years ago.

"If you can call it that," she said. "I was clearly ahead."

"It was a competition." Aneel grinned. "And I don't think so. We were neck and neck until the final competition."

"Desserts," Karina spat out with an exaggerated eye roll for the cameras. She started boiling milk for the kulfi and took out the spices she wanted to use for flavoring.

"Desserts are not Chef Mistry's forte," Aneel threw out with a smirk.

"Of course, sugar would be Chef Rawal's strong suit. How hard is it to toss sugar on something and have people like it?" Karina asked the room.

"Not hard for me," he stage-whispered. "But some people..." He tilted his head toward Karina.

"Some people like to create something," Karina said. "While others..." she jutted her chin at him and caught his eye. Her heart gave a thud, and she forgot how to speak. Silence lay heavy in the kitchen for a beat too long. She caught herself "...while others just dip everything in simple syrup and present it as dessert." She chuckled.

"Who won?" Divya Shah asked from off camera.

Aneel smiled wide into the camera.

"Well, Chef Rawal, over there did, didn't he?" Karina had to force some animosity into her voice, because she found that it was no longer naturally there. She did not care who won that darned thing. Or how.

"Although, Chef Mistry over here..." he flicked a thumb at her while he worked "...was so distraught over losing, she—"

"Ate his dessert." She widened her eyes at him. He was

clearly going to mention that she had accused him of cheating. This was not the place for that. For either of them.

Divya gasped. "Is this true?"

Karina laughed. "I waited until after the competition, but he had made the most beautiful jalebi. Perfect spirals, crisp bite, but soft on the inside, and the hardest part of jalebi—it was the perfect balance of sweet with a hint of tart." She rolled her eyes into her head. "Divine." She paused. "So I ate one. Maybe two."

Karina caught Aneel glancing at her as he worked, clearly puzzled. She felt his eyes on her, and she spared him a glance before she looked directly into the camera. "They were amazing."

"I had no idea that you'd even tried them." Aneel's voice was soft from his side of the kitchen.

Deepak glared at her. They were being nice to each other. She pressed her lips together. "It was considered the good sportsmanship thing to do. We all tried each other's desserts."

He seemed to catch himself. "Well then, I guess today you get another chance to prove your dessert making abilities."

"You got it, Chef Rawal." Karina put on her evil grin. "Enough chatter, Chef. I have your ass to kick."

Aneel shook his head at Karina as he continued to work. "Bring it, *Chef.*"

Chapter Twenty-One

Divya Shah, pastry chef, business owner, maker of some of the best Indian and honestly, some non-Indian desserts in the city and one of his culinary heroes, announced him the winner that night, and Aneel thought he would die on the spot.

The next thing he knew, Karina's arms were around him, and she was laughing. Everything happened in slow motion. Her citrus scent was heaven, and he couldn't help but melt a little into her body. He hadn't realized how badly he wanted to hold her until he was doing just that. And she was holding him back and beaming at him. It really was the most perfect moment.

When she pulled away, he felt the loss like a physical blow. The flush on her face and the shock in her eyes only enhanced her beauty, even though she stepped back as if in hugging him she had done something wrong. His body ached to have her back in his arms, but she stepped away as the judges approached to congratulate him.

Aneel had turned again to look for Karina when he spotted his sister.

"Hey," Saira said as the crew started packing up and the staff began to clean up.

"Hey." Relief flooded him at the sight of the most important person in his life. He had never been awkward with his sister before. Even in her teenage years. This was terrible. "Um, let's go to the office."

She nodded and followed him. He hadn't seen her in a week. He was trying to give her the space Tyler had said she needed, not to mention the space he needed, too. He still hated the empty apartment, but he had taken the emptiness as an opportunity to reflect.

"I'm sorry I was such an overbearing, overprotective brother," he said once they were alone. "I worry about you."

"It's who you are, Bhaiya," she said lightly, a small smile coming to her face. She looked more like their mother every day. "I wasn't trying to hurt you. But we don't have to agree on everything."

He smiled inwardly. *Agree to disagree.* "I just… I want you to be careful, Saira. He's dangerous." Reflection had not changed his mind about their father.

"He's not," she insisted, lifting her chin to him.

"You've continued to meet with him." Aneel met his sister's eyes. So much like their mother's.

She nodded. "He explained everything."

"How do you know it's true?"

"I'm trusting him. Taking a chance, I guess." She fixed him in her gaze.

"Huge chance, little sister."

"I'm not so little anymore." The conviction in her voice backed up her statement.

Aneel nodded. That much was apparent. Tears burned behind his eyes. "I miss you."

"Me, too." Her voice broke.

Aneel gathered her up in his arms and held her tight. She was still everything to him. She wrapped her arms around him. She still loved him, too.

"I've seen you bickering with Karina on TV," she said as she pulled back and wiped her eyes.

"The bickering, it's for the show. She's actually… Well, she's actually very nice and kind. She has a son."

"She's married?"

"Divorced."

"Well, that makes sense." Saira rolled her eyes.

"She's... It's not like that. We misjudged her back then," Aneel said.

"You're giving Karina Mistry a second chance, but you won't talk to Dad?" Saira seemed more amused than irritated.

Aneel pressed his lips into a line. "It's not the same thing."

Saira shrugged but nodded. It was not.

"You're not coming home, are you?" Aneel asked quietly.

"I'm still finalizing a place. It's time for me to move out. I need to be closer to school. I need my own space, Bhaiya," she said quietly.

Aneel nodded. "I know. It's about time you stopped mooching off of me anyway. Cramping my style."

She smirked at him. "I supposed you'll have women over all the time now, huh?"

"All. The. Time."

"As if." Tyler huffed from the door.

"I could have women over all the time if I wanted," Aneel mock-bragged to his friend.

Tyler frowned and nodded his head vigorously as if humoring a child. "Sure you can, buddy. Sure, you can."

"Shut up. I don't see you dating all the time, either." Aneel reverted to the seventh-grade version of himself that seemed to surface when he was around Tyler.

"I have been dating a woman." He grinned.

Saira rolled her eyes. "I've been there over a week and I have never seen her. You never even mentioned her."

"I don't tell you everything." Tyler started to defend himself.

"You didn't tell me either," Aneel said.

Saira smirked. "I need to get to the clinic." She stepped

toward the door. "Tyler, thanks for the ride. I'm going back home until my new place is finalized."

"Sounds good," Tyler replied, his gaze lingering on her a moment longer than necessary.

"I'll see you tonight, Bhaiya." Saira smiled and waved.

Aneel sighed, relief flooding every muscle and cell in his body. It was good to have his sister back.

"Who is the mystery woman?" Aneel asked.

"An attorney I met a few weeks ago. Beautiful, super smart. But we're both busy, so we've only been out a few times." Tyler shrugged. "What about you and the Chef?"

"What about us?" Aneel feigned attention for the paperwork on the desk.

"Your chemistry is off the charts. That's why the producers are so happy," Tyler said.

"That's just for the show." Aneel waved it off. There was no way Karina had any real feelings for him, was there?

"You can't fake that. You're nowhere near that good an actor. And likely, neither is she."

Aneel looked at his friend.

Tyler's jaw dropped. "You do like her."

"She has a son."

"Yeah?" Tyler furrowed his brow, the lawyer in him coming out. "Where's the dad?"

"No idea. They divorced before Veer was born." Aneel shook his head at the thought of Veer and grinned. "Loves Avengers and debating who the best one is."

"Who? Chef or the kid?"

Aneel chuckled. "Both."

"Lock it in."

"What the hell are you saying, 'lock it in'? Is that how you talk now?"

"I'm saying, you two seem really good together, and she's amazing. Do not let her get away."

"You don't even know her," Aneel insisted.

"Who doesn't know who?" Karina's voice came from the door.

Aneel's heart nearly stopped as he shot a look at Tyler. Had he known Karina was right there?

"Ah... Tyler claims to be dating, but I don't think there's a woman who would actually date his sorry ass," Aneel said, trying to cover the shake in his voice.

Karina shook her head at him, then turned to look at Tyler. She drew her gaze over him, head to toe. "Chef Rawal," she said, drawing out the word and pulling her gaze from Tyler to Aneel. "You are mistaken. There are any number of women who would date Tyler."

Tyler grinned at him from behind Karina as something ugly twisted in Aneel's belly. He had a very strong urge to punch Tyler.

"That is the nicest thing anyone has said to me in a long time, Karina." Tyler grinned like a Cheshire cat. He made a show of leaning down and kissing Karina's cheek as he winked at Aneel. "I'm free for dinner tonight. We could go—"

"No. You aren't," Aneel snapped. "You have a date with the lawyer."

"Right." Tyler wiggled his eyebrows over a knowing look. The effect was entirely irritating. "I need to get to the office. Great show." He threw one more look at Aneel as he left.

Karina stared at Aneel a moment. "Everything okay?"

"Huh? Yeah. Just Tyler." Aneel shook his head.

"How did it go with Saira?" she asked, settling into the small sofa in the office.

He sat down next to her. "We talked. She still wants to move out." He shrugged. "It's time. She'll be a veterinarian in less than a year."

"What about your dad?" Karina turned to face him, putting all of her energy and attention on him. She pulled one leg onto the sofa, and it grazed his thigh. She had taken her hair out of the net. The bun was still intact, but a few loose tendrils framed her face.

"She wants to give him a chance. I think it's a mistake." Aneel turned his body so he faced her, their legs touching. He chuckled. "We have to agree to disagree."

She laughed. "Veer gives good advice."

Aneel sighed in resignation. "She's going to graduate, she's getting her own place, making her own decisions. She's all grown up." His heart ached as he realized that his job as her parent was basically done.

"You get to just be her big brother now." Karina pressed her leg against his in a show of camaraderie.

He shook his head, his heart heavy. "I don't even know what that means."

"Well, if Param and his brothers are any example—which they may not be—brothers basically tease without mercy." She smiled, and it was a beautiful sight. Sure, she still had on the makeup for the camera. But it wasn't her features he noticed. Her smile as she thought about the Sheth brothers was filled with humor and love. Her eyes sparkled with amusement. "But…" and her eyes reflected love again "…they have always had my back. When Chirag—my ex-husband—left, Nishant wanted to chase after him to the Himalayas and beat the you-know-what out of him." She chuckled. "God help Chirag, if Nishant ever finds him."

"I can do that. I can be that guy for Saira," Aneel said with a laugh.

Karina rested her head on the sofa, still watching him, a small smile on her face. "It might not be easy, Aneel, but it can be done."

He met her gaze and became hyperaware of her leg against his. The air changed, electrified, as she held his gaze. He moved toward her, and she lifted her head, alert to his movements, but didn't move away. Her eyes softened, and her lips parted, beckoning him closer.

"That's good to know, Karina," his words came out low, like he was afraid to lose the moment. He felt her lean toward him, her breath catching. Her gaze dropped to his mouth, heating him. They were close enough that her breath mingled with his, her citrus scent surrounding and filling him. "Karina."

"Mmm." She leaned closer.

He moved toward her, the taste of her lips just a breath away. "Chef Rawal."

Karina whipped away from him with speed worthy of an Avenger as Jacob knocked on the door.

"Jacob," Aneel breathed, trying and failing not to glance at Karina. "What's up?"

"Deepak is looking for you. To go over the menu for the week?"

"Right." Aneel inhaled and stood. "I'll be right out."

"Sure." Jacob left.

Karina stood as well and was already at the door. "I need to get Veer."

"Karina—"

She flushed. "I...really need to go." She was gone before he could say anything else.

He plopped himself back onto the sofa. His phone buzzed. A text from Tyler.

You kissed her, right?

If only he had.

Chapter Twenty-Two

Karina didn't even bother taking off her whites in the locker room. She had no idea what had almost happened on that sofa.

Not true.

She knew exactly what almost happened. She had been about to kiss Aneel. If Jacob hadn't come in, she would one hundred percent be making out with Aneel right now. Which would be—

What would it be? Amazing, fantastic. Irresponsible. Ridiculous.

She grabbed her backpack and her purse and headed out the back door of the restaurant as fast as she could without letting it appear as if she were in a hurry. She didn't stop until she was in her car. Her breath came hard and fast, and she rested her head against the steering wheel.

What had she almost done? She couldn't be making out with men she'd only just met.

Technically, she met him seven years ago. That was it. She snapped her head up. She had been ready to kiss him because of that latent attraction she'd had for him back then. It wasn't anything real. It wasn't like she had feelings for him *at the moment*.

Because having feelings for him right now would not work. She had a young son. She had to be careful who she brought in to not only her life but his life as well. So, make-out sessions on the office sofa were off-limits. Right. Good.

She inhaled and exhaled, feeling much calmer now. She started the car.

She was simultaneously thrilled and guilt ridden by how excited Veer was when he saw her car. That was motherhood, both those feelings all the time.

Veer hopped into the car seat in the back, and his teacher buckled him.

"Hi, sweetie," Karina greeted him. "What do you want to do today?"

His eyes bugged out. "No cooking?"

She smiled in the rearview. "I'm taking the day off. You and me. Whatever you wish." She did not have a menu to plan for the week, and the catering could wait a few hours.

"Make forts?" he asked, clearly doubting that she would agree.

"Sure."

"Pizza for dinner?" he asked. "From outside."

"Okay. Takeout pizza." She dragged out the words like she didn't really want to. "But only if we can watch Avengers movies!"

"Well, Mom." He dragged his words out as she just had, his dark eyes glowing with mischief. "If you really want to watch Avengers movies, then I can do that with you."

Sarcasm. She shook her head. Her kid was learning sarcasm.

They got home and changed into comfy clothes. It was too early for pizza, so she made them popcorn and mixed in peanut M&M's before they gathered all the pillows and blankets to make his fort.

Veer talked nonstop while they assembled the fort. The subjects ranged from his friends at school to the Avengers and everything in between.

He quieted down as they put on the finishing touches. "Mom? If I had a dad, there would be plenty of room in the fort for him."

Her heart fell into her stomach. "Do you want a dad?"

"Everyone wants a dad," he said. "Except for Molly. She has two moms, and she says that is enough parents." He crunched his popcorn.

"But do you want one?"

He shrugged. "Sometimes it might be fun. Sonia said she didn't have a mom for a while. But then her dad got married, and now she has a mom. She really likes her. You could do that."

"Do what?"

"Get married, and then I would have a dad."

She turned to face him. "And what kind of dad should I get you?"

Veer turned to her to count on his fingers again. "He has to like the Avengers. I'm okay if his favorite is different than mine."

"Okay. Avengers. What else?"

He held up two fingers. "He should be big and strong to fight the bad guys." He held up three fingers. "And he should be funny. And I want him to like to play with me."

"That's it?"

Veer was silent for a while. "He could be like Aneel Uncle."

Karina froze. "You met him like two times."

"Yeah. But I watch him on your show. And I know you're fake fighting."

"Wait, how do you know that?" She leaned toward her little man and all this insight in such a cute little package.

"Because." He rolled his little eyes. "I see you real fighting with Sona Masi and Rani Masi."

She chuckled at him and popped an M&M in her mouth. "Yeah. Okay. Fair."

"Aneel Uncle would be a good dad."

She stared at her son. She had no idea if Aneel would be a good father or not. She really had not thought about it. All the more reason she should not go around kissing him. She sighed in relief that she had not, Veer's preferences aside.

"Okay. Are we watching Captain America or what?"

"Yes," he said, sitting back to lean on his pillow. "See how cool Captain America is? Aneel Uncle doesn't get it." He pressed his lips together and gave a shake of his head.

As if on cue, someone knocked at the mudroom door. Only one person knocked. Everyone else just came in. She started to get up, butterflies in her stomach, wondering why he was here.

Veer hopped up first. "Aneel Uncle!" Even he knew who knocked at the door.

She paused the movie—Veer liked to see *everything*—and stood to follow him.

"Aneel Uncle." Veer's voice came from the mudroom. "You're just in time to watch Captain America with me and Mom."

"Hey, Veer." Aneel's rumble reached her from the mudroom and still managed to hit her in her core. She exhaled. "I don't think I—"

"Mom!" Veer called, ignoring Aneel's protest as he walked into the kitchen. "Aneel Uncle is going to watch Captain America with us. Right?" He turned to Aneel.

Aneel looked from Veer to her, looking torn. Her heart thudded hard and fast. "Well, I just came to talk to your mom. But if you're watching Captain America, we can talk tomorrow."

"But you're here already," Veer insisted. He motioned for Aneel to bend down. Aneel knelt so Veer could whisper. "She's letting me have pizza—from *outside*."

Karina heard her son clearly, a smile coming to her mouth. Until Aneel looked up at her. Those brown eyes simmered with everything that had and had not happened. She swallowed and looked away, unable to face what his gaze was doing to her.

Aneel turned to Veer. "How about you have some time, just you and Mom? I'll catch up with her tomorrow."

"But the movie…" Veer looked from Aneel to her. He didn't understand what was happening.

Karina cleared her throat and found her voice. "Aneel Uncle is welcome to stay," she said, then turned her gaze to him. "If he wants. It's just Captain America and pizza."

"Right." Aneel clenched his jaw but nodded his understanding. This was for Veer, and Veer only. He turned to Veer, a huge smile on his face. Showing off those dimples and everything. "Looks like Chef says yes!" he said excitedly. He took off his coat and hung it in the mudroom, leaving his shoes there as well. "Are we watching Captain America's origin story, because that's where we should start."

"Yes," Veer said, grabbing Aneel's hand and leading him to the fort.

Karina followed. Aneel turned back to look at her. She kept her face unreadable, though his was clear. He had wanted to talk about what happened on the sofa. Or maybe what didn't happen.

Thankfully, Veer plopped down in the middle of the fort. Karina took her seat next to him, and Aneel took the seat on Veer's other side.

"I'm ordering the pizza. What do you want?" Karina asked as she took out her phone.

"Onions, mushrooms and pepperoni." Both males spoke in unison.

She gaped at them as they gaped at each other. She knew that was Veer's order, but… Aneel caught her eye and gave her a one-shoulder shrug. What were the odds?

"I knew we were buddies," Veer said excitedly. Karina just stared at him. He pushed Play, and the movie started.

Karina was all too aware of Aneel sitting on the other side of her son, the two of them discussing the minutiae of the movie. Veer was little, hardly a separation between them. She inhaled deeply, completely aware of Aneel's spice-and-leather scent. She glanced over and found him looking at her. She looked away.

"You okay, Mom?"

"Hmm? Yeah, I'm fine."

"You did that thing you do when someone irritates you."

"Did I?" She caught Aneel's eye. "I hadn't noticed."

"That's okay. I know you don't like the other guys in the barracks making fun of Steve," Veer said.

"Right. That's what it was."

The pizza arrived, and she brought over wine for her and Aneel and a mini soda can for Veer. They ate straight from the box in the fort.

Veer gave commentary every so often. Aneel did not back down from Iron Man, but the discussion was lively as they watched the movie. Karina insisted she thought Hulk was the best, which resulted in both Aneel and Veer shaking their heads at her in pity.

"Come on. He's a scientist, no ego, and he finds a way to have both parts of him in one. Plus he's green."

"That's a plus?" Aneel asked.

"Of course. No one else is green."

"Gamora is," Veer said.

"Right. Whatever. You're both still both wrong," Karina said. She could feel them both rolling their eyes at each other.

Her father came home around 7:30 p.m. and joined them under the fort at Veer's insistence but refused the pizza. He cut his eyes to Aneel and raised an eyebrow at Karina, but she ignored him. He was curious about Aneel hanging out with Veer. She had no answers.

The movie finished, and Karina stood, holding out her hand to Veer. "Bedtime, kiddo. School tomorrow."

"But we didn't watch Iron Man!"

"Well, we can't watch all of them today, anyway," Karina told him. This wasn't supposed to become a regular thing.

"If it's okay with your mom, I'll watch Iron Man with you another time," Aneel offered.

"Next Monday?" asked Veer.

"Aneel Uncle and I are catering that day." She glanced at him.

"How about Sunday?" her father suggested. "No school Monday."

Karina shot her father a look. What was he doing?

"Sounds like a plan," Aneel said. He held his palm out to Veer. "Good night. See you on Sunday."

Veer high-fived him. There were over thirty movies in this franchise. Karina should be panicked.

Somehow, she was not. Suddenly thirty movies did not seem like that many. Suddenly, they didn't seem like enough.

Aneel waited in the kitchen while Karina put Veer to bed. He did his best to chat amiably with Sachin Uncle without appearing to be going out of his mind. He needed to talk to her.

"Staring at the steps will not make her come down faster," Uncle said to him, his eyebrows raised.

"Oh. I wasn't… I mean—"

Uncle just shook his head at him.

Aneel sighed and stopped fighting it. "Okay."

As if a reward for his honesty, Karina came down the stairs. She walked past him and her father right to far end of the kitchen. She pulled out the dough she must have made earlier for the little pani puri. A challenging task for sure, making the bite-sized fried shells.

Sachin Uncle looked at him. "I'm heading out," he said. "Meeting."

"Kind of late for a meeting, isn't it?" Karina asked as she slowly kneaded the dough.

"Kind of late to be making puri, isn't it?" her father countered.

"Enjoy your meeting, Uncle," Aneel said.

"Enjoy...making puri," Uncle said with a small smirk as he left.

Aneel turned to find Karina watching him. "I'm good to do the puri," she said. "You have to run the restaurant. Go home. Get some sleep."

"It'll get done faster with both of us working. All those small little puri, and you have to get the right amount of crunch."

"I always get the right amount of crunch," she said with a small smirk.

"Let's see then," Aneel said.

Karina took a golf ball-sized piece of dough and started rolling it out, then took a one-inch round cookie cutter and cut out the smaller puri. Aneel grabbed a rolling pin and followed suit. She turned on the old Bollywood songs they had in common, but outside of that, she wouldn't even look at him.

They worked in silence for a while. Aneel switched to frying when they had rolled out enough dough that both tasks could be done in tandem.

Sure enough, each small puri puffed into a crispy shell, ready to be stuffed and eaten.

"Perfect crunch," he said.

Just then, a drop of water fell from the ceiling to the floor, right behind Karina, quickly followed by couple more drops. He mopped it up with a towel. "Karina. What's above this?"

She looked up at the ceiling. "Master bath."

"I think it's leaking."

She sighed. "Bucket in the mudroom. It's happened before. I'll call the plumber in the morning."

He went and grabbed the bucket, and they continued to work in silence for a bit.

"Karina," he started, his voice soft.

She kept working.

"Karina. About what happened today."

"Nothing happened today." She kept her concentration on the rolling pin, her voice overly casual. Like if she didn't acknowledge it, it would all go away.

That would not fly with him. "That's not true, and you know it. If Jacob hadn't walked in—"

"If Jacob hadn't walked in, we would have kissed, and that would have been a terrible mistake," she blurted out.

"Are you sure?" he asked.

"Am I sure what?" The touch of irritation in her voice was fast becoming one of his favorite things.

"Are you sure that I would have kissed you?" He smirked.

Her eyes fired up, and it was a thing of beauty. "Are you saying you wouldn't have?"

He shrugged. "I'm not saying one way or the other. Jacob walked in, and now we'll never know, will we? Unless you're saying that you would have kissed me."

Karina furrowed her brow. She opened her mouth, then shut it, clearly at a loss.

"So why don't you tell me why kissing me would have been such a terrible mistake that you can't even talk to me right now?"

Karina went back to rolling out puris. "I can't just go around kissing random men. No matter how sunny their disposition."

"I'm wounded, Grumpy. I am not a random man." God, he really hoped he wasn't. That might be worse than not kissing her. What? He hadn't even kissed her and he wanted to be more than just a random guy to her? He sank into the realization that he wanted to *matter* to her.

"Well, no." She continued to work. "Kissing can lead to other things—I don't want you to think we're just going to hop into bed."

"I would not have expected you to sleep with me just because we kissed." But now he was thinking about having sex with her. He shook his head. *Focus!* "I don't know who you've been dating, but if a woman decides to sleep with me, it's her decision. Not mine."

She glanced at him. "Right. And I haven't been dating." She pressed her lips tightly together.

"Really?"

"Not since the divorce. I don't want to be in a relationship. I have Veer to think about."

"Kissing me also does not equal a relationship." He inhaled. "I have a list of women who can attest to that. Starting with Meg Shannon in second grade. One smooch under the slide, and she thought we were getting married." He shook his head and exhaled. "It got ugly."

This earned him a smile and an eye roll. "You're funny, Sunshine. I'll give you that."

"But that's all? Not even…friends?" Tyler would punch him right now for friend-zoning himself. But he was ready to take friendship if that was all she could do. He was ready to accept any part of her she was willing to share.

"I'll consider friends," she said softly.

"Tough crowd." He lifted his hand to tuck back a stray tendril of hair. But stopped short of grazing his fingers on her cheek, though he knew her skin would feel like silk.

She cleared her throat and stepped back. "Fine, Sunshine. Get back to work, these puri are not going to fry themselves."

Chapter Twenty-Three

About an hour into puri making, Karina and Aneel had fallen into debating the best way to make dhal. Their moms' Bollywood songs played in the background. The current song was the male lead singing about how the smile of his love interest had opened up dreams for him.

Karina found herself singing along quietly as they argued the various ways that dhal could be made. She and Aneel were in agreement on one thing—they did not like the addition of sweetness in their dhal, typical Gujarati cooking or not.

Aneel slowly added the small uncooked dough discs to the hot oil. "I get adding a bit of gor to bring out the other flavors—"

"But I don't want to taste the jaggery sweetness," Karina finished on a laugh.

He smiled at her, and it took everything she had not to kiss that mouth. Thankfully, that was when Sona made her appearance.

"Oh, the OG Bollywood songs!" Sona sang along for a line or two. She walked over to the sink to grab some water. "What's with the bucket?"

Karina flushed and went back to rolling puri. "The tub in the master bathroom is leaking again. I'll call the plumber in the morning."

"Or I could do that," Sona said as she grabbed a finished shell and popped it in her mouth with a satisfied crunch.

"Oh no, that's fine. I'll do it," Karina said.

"Why do you do that?" Sona asked.

"What?"

"Take charge, take everything on you. I'm home tomorrow. I am fully capable of calling the plumber." Sona stared at her.

"You want to call the plumber?"

"Well, nobody *wants* to call the plumber. But you're busy with all this and Veer." Sona raised her eyebrows at her. "I'm not a child anymore, Karina Ben. I don't need you to take care of me," she finished softly.

Karina just stared at her sister for a moment. She was right. Sona was fully capable of taking care of the house. "Okay. We have a contract with—"

"My god, Karina Ben. I got it." Sona shook her head at Aneel in frustration as she popped another puri in her mouth. "These are fab, by the way. You two make a great team."

Karina felt Aneel's gaze land on her. "That we do," he said. "Almost like we're friends."

"Uh. Are you not friends?" Sona asked slowly.

"Not according to your sister," Aneel stated.

"Ah." Sona nodded, amusement on her face. "Yeah. She's tough that way."

"I could be a friend," Aneel pressed.

Sona grinned at Aneel. "Okay. Give me your argument."

Karina glared at her sister. What the hell?

Aneel held up one finger while he continued frying. "One. Friends have things in common. We are both chefs." He held up two fingers. "Two. Friends help each other. I am helping her with the chai masala." He turned to Karina and gave her a gentle look. "You helped me the other day at work."

"That was self-preservation, Sunshine," she said.

Three fingers now. "Three. Friends enjoy each other's company. She has clearly enjoyed hanging out with me here and at work. I know this because she smiles, and she does not slam the door in my face. And four—friends give each other nicknames. Right, Grumpy?" He wiggled his eyebrows at her.

She groaned. Aneel just stared at her a moment, his jaw slack before shaking his head and snapping out of it.

"He makes a good argument, Karina Ben." Sona grinned at her. The traitor turned to Aneel and offered her hand. "Welcome to the family, Aneel. Hopefully you won't regret taking on Karina as a friend. You understand that we all come with that package?"

Aneel chuckled and looked at Karina. "I'm counting on it."

Karina scowled and looked up at Aneel, only to find him looking at her, victory in his eyes. Something in her chest loosened, and her traitorous gaze dropped to his mouth. She flicked her eyes right back up to his and saw them darken.

"Fine," she conceded. "We're friends."

Sona chuckled. "Where's Papa?"

"He went to some meeting," Karina said, intently frying the puri.

"That was like three hours ago," Aneel said, his voice a bit gravelly.

"You okay?" asked Sona. "Need water?"

He flicked his gaze to Karina. "I'm just fine."

Karina snapped her head up at him. He was paying attention to her father's comings and goings?

"Oh." Sona chuckled. "He's not at a meeting."

"Then where is he?" Karina asked.

"He's on a *date*," Aneel said, pointedly looking at Sona. "Isn't he?"

"I'm not supposed to say." Her sister grinned.

"Why not?" Karina fired up.

"Because Rani said not to bug you with all that while you were competing for this job. That you would freak out and not do well at work," Sona replied.

"That is so not true. Wait till I see Rani. I'm not going to freak out. Why would I freak out just because my seventy-year-old widowed father is going on a date with a woman we know nothing about?"

"We know her. She's so cool."

Karina's eyes bugged out. "You've met her?"

"Oh no," Sona said. "I'm going to bed."

"Oh no, you're not. Tell me." Karina narrowed her eyes at her sister.

"Fine. Her name is Rupa. She's a doctor in family practice. They met at a conference. We met her briefly one night when she came to pick up Papa for dinner. You were at work."

"How long has this been going on?" Karina asked. How long had her family been keeping this from her?

"Like a few weeks. Maybe a month."

"He's been seeing her for a month, and I'm just finding out now?"

"You know how you are." Sona grabbed a slice of pizza.

"Do tell."

"Overprotective. Nosy."

"I am not nosy."

"But you admit you're overprotective. Ha!" Sona grinned at her.

"Whatever." Karina pressed her lips together. Somebody had to make sure that everyone in the family was okay. Couldn't just let a seventy-year-old man run around dating random women.

"Your dad is fine," Aneel said as if he'd been reading her mind.

"We don't know anything about this woman," Karina said.

"That is okay. He's a grown man."

"I don't like it."

"Exactly why your sisters didn't tell you."

Chapter Twenty-Four

"Just come to the apartment, and we'll work on it there. It's fine," Aneel insisted to Karina. They were finishing up at the restaurant on a slow Wednesday. She had just gotten a message from Sona. The drywall in the ceiling of the kitchen had been removed where the leak was, but they wouldn't fix that until the leak was fixed. Basically, she couldn't use her kitchen safely for a few days.

She just looked at him, her luscious lips pressed together as she considered his offer.

"It's not as big, but I do have the gas stove and decent counter space. We can manage."

"There's no school tomorrow. Veer—"

"Can come over and hang out with us if you need him to." Aneel was very excited at the prospect of having Karina at his place, but he really needed to clean before she came over.

"Okay. I guess there's no choice." She finally gave in.

"See? This is what friends are for, Grumpy."

She shook her head at him. "Point taken, Sunshine."

He wiggled his eyebrows at her and was rewarded with a small eye roll and a blush. He picked up his phone. "Here's the address. Come whenever in the morning."

"Thank you." She nodded and went back to wiping down counters. Aneel wanted to tell her to go home, but he knew she would not, so he helped her.

He texted Saira. Karina is coming over to cook in the morning. She's bringing her son. Clean up!

Saira did not respond. Fine, he'd clean before he went to bed.

Karina texted before she came over with Veer around 8:00 a.m.

"Hey, Veer." Aneel jutted his chin at the little boy as they entered the apartment.

"Hey, Aneel Uncle." He glanced at the TV. *Iron Man* was on. "Awesome!"

"I see you brought your mom with you." Aneel rolled his eyes.

Veer's face lit up, and he giggled. "I have to. I'm only four. I don't know how to get places."

Aneel nodded in understanding. "Sure, sure. I get that. You hungry?"

Veer nodded. "She didn't feed me."

Aneel shook his head in disbelief. "She's a mom. Isn't she supposed to feed you?" He glanced at Karina as she watched her son. The smile on her face warmed his heart.

Veer shrugged.

"Lucky your mom has a friend like me." He made eye contact with Karina and grinned. "I made you my famous eggs." He put some in a bowl and settled Veer in a chair with Iron Man.

Veer eagerly dug in, humming in delight after sampling his first bite. "Mom. Learn how to make the famous eggs. I love them."

Karina shook her head at Aneel. "Now I need to learn famous eggs."

Aneel leaned toward her, taking in her fabulous citrus scent. "You're a trained chef. I think you can handle it."

She met his gaze, only inches from his face and his heart stopped at those hazel eyes. Not just the beauty, but the spark of longing that flitted through them. He stifled a groan. She swallowed. "We should…"

"Right." He backed away from her and they got to work on the paratha. Karina had made the dough at home and brought it with her, so they needed to roll out the spiced flatbread and pan roast with oil—and repeat that two hundred times.

They were well on their way when Saira came home, holding a small animal carrier. Saira had not in fact cleaned and had left early this morning without saying a word. Aneel assumed it was because she wasn't a fan of Karina's.

"Oh, hey." Saira looked at Karina, her gaze drifting over to where to Veer sat, engrossed in his movie, eating a second bowl of eggs. "I…uh…didn't think anyone would be home."

"I texted you last night," Aneel said.

"My phone died, and I haven't caught up on texts."

A small bark came from the carrier. Saira's eyes widened. Veer turned toward the door, and Karina's eyes lit up.

"What was that?" Veer asked.

Aneel narrowed his eyes at his sister. "Yes, do tell."

Veer walked over. "Who are you?"

"Veer, this my sister, Saira. She's going to be an animal doctor. Saira. This is Veer Mistry."

Veer extended his hand. Saira shook it. "Nice to meet you, Auntie."

"Yeah, you, too, kid." Saira looked around the room. "Well, you look busy. I'll just go to my room."

She took one step before Veer asked, "Is there a dog in there?"

Saira inhaled, looking at her brother. "There might be."

"Saira!" Aneel shook his head at her.

His call of indignation was drowned out by Karina's squeal of delight. "Ooh! Can we see?"

Saira appeared shocked. "Um, yes. Okay." She looked at Aneel. "She just came into the shelter today."

Before Aneel could completely process, Saira had opened the carrier and pulled out a beautiful puppy. Both Karina and Veer plopped themselves on the floor to play with the tiny little dog. Veer was bonkers for the dog as she climbed on him and sniffed and licked. His giggles echoed in the small apartment.

But it was Karina who took his breath away. The look of unadulterated joy on her face as the puppy greeted her with licks and sniffs and tail wags was something he had never seen before.

"Aww. She's adorable. I love the brindle color." Karina studied the dog. "She looks like a mix." Her face was glowing.

Saira looked surprised. "Um. Yeah. She is a mix, we think dachshund, maybe terrier."

Karina petted the puppy who was currently curled up in her lap. "I always wanted a dog. My sisters and I all did. We researched, and I did a whole presentation, and our parents were like the only parents on the planet who didn't fall for it." She shrugged, her attention still on the puppy, stroking her fur.

"Same. I did a whole presentation for my mom, and my brother said he didn't want a dog. That he didn't like animals. Then he said, 'Become a vet.' So here we are." Saira was starting to relax a bit with Karina, but Aneel could see she was still uncomfortable.

"Fine. Just potty train her." Aneel managed a small scowl.

"Yes, Bhaiya. Right." Saira picked up the puppy and placed her back in the carrier. "I'll just take her in my room. I have to study." She straightened and waved to the room. "Nice to meet you, Veer."

Veer waved as well, and Saira disappeared down the small hallway to her room.

"Aneel Uncle?"

"Yeah?"

"Your sister seems sad about something."

Aneel looked at Karina, who shrugged, not really surprised by her son's statement. "All right. I'll talk to her later."

"I think she wants to keep that dog."

Aneel chuckled low. "You may be right."

Veer went back to his movie. Karina began to wash up, and they went back to their rhythm.

"I had no idea that Grumpy had a soft spot for puppies," Aneel drawled at her.

"Everyone has a soft spot for puppies." Karina gave him a crooked smile. "Except for you, apparently. Almost scandalous."

"I love animals. And I have a very soft spot for puppies," he whispered, glancing down the hall where his sister was studying.

"But your sister just said…" Karina elbowed him.

He sighed. "Things were tight. Dogs cost money. Mom was already working too much. Saira was only seven, and she wouldn't have understood that." He felt Karina stop rolling out dough and look at him. He maintained his focus straight ahead. "Do not feel sorry for me, Grumpy. I don't think I could take it."

"No. That's not it," she said softly.

He turned to look at her. Sure enough, it was not pity he found on her face, it was pride. Her hazel eyes were glassy as she smiled at him. "You are a very good big brother, Aneel Rawal. In case no one told you recently."

He flipped over the paratha and drizzled oil onto it before he looked at her again. A small smile creeped onto his face as a small part of his heart loosened and lightened. "Thank you." He nodded his head and continued to work. "Thank you."

Chapter Twenty-Five

Karina was at Aneel's apartment by 8:00 a.m. the following day, as Sona was home to take Veer to school.

They had indeed made progress yesterday, but if they could get the sweets done, that would be even better. Mini gulab jamun was on deck today, and it could be time-consuming.

It had nothing to do with wanting to see him.

Nothing at all.

She was going to buzz the door for entry from the outside of the building, but an older Indian woman was just entering and allowed Karina in. The woman smiled kindly as they waited for the elevator. They both got off on Aneel's floor. Karina walked to his apartment and raised a hand to knock.

"Beti," the woman said. "You know Aneel Rawal?"

Karina smiled. "We work together."

"Hanh. Achha. Okay." The woman kept walking and entered another apartment.

Karina knocked.

Aneel came to the door but did not open it all the way. "Hey." He seemed surprised to see her.

"Hey," she said. "I thought we were meeting this morning?"

"We were. We are. Uh…did I know you were coming this early?" he asked.

Karina's eyes widened, and her heart fell into her stomach. Crap. He had someone in there. Someone who must have been there all night, because only crazy women like her showed up at 8:00 a.m. to cook.

"Um. I don't know. We're making mini—actually never mind. You clearly have someone in there, and I'm interrupting." Oh god, she was going to be sick. Or she was going to cry which really made no sense at all, because why the hell should she care if Aneel had a *sleepover* with a woman? He was free to do whoever—whatever—he wanted. They were just friends, colleagues.

That was what she told him she wanted.

She turned to leave before she further embarrassed herself.

"Karina. Wait." He glanced behind him. "Just come in. It's not what you think."

"Isn't it?"

"You're thinking that I had a woman over last night."

She stared at him. "Well. Maybe."

"Aneel, beta. Everything okay?" The voice of an older Indian woman with a slight accent came from inside his apartment.

Karina sagged in relief. "Oh! You have an auntie in there." She brushed past him and into the apartment.

Sure enough there was an auntie sitting at the small breakfast bar. Next to her was probably the most beautiful woman Karina had ever seen. She froze. This was worse than a sleepover. She had no idea why it was worse than a sleepover, but somehow it felt worse than a sleepover.

Aneel came up behind her, his hand resting gently on the small of her back. Any other time, she might have melted right into that touch. But right now, she was torn between fuming and crying. The touch felt like an apology. But she wasn't sure why she needed one.

"Karina, this is Toral, and her masi, Tara Auntie. Karina and I work together," he told them.

Right. They were colleagues. Maybe friends.

"Oh, I've seen you on that show," Toral said, her eyes widening in admiration. "I love the banter. Very cute. And the food just looks so amazing!"

"She doesn't watch much TV," Tara Auntie said. "She is busy as a surgeon."

Toral pressed her mouth into a line and inhaled deeply. "Masi, please."

"What? You are a doctor. They should know. Aneel..." Tara Auntie grinned widely at him, her face full of affection "...should know."

"You've told him ten times. Besides, I'm a pediatrician. Not a surgeon," Toral said, clearly reaching the end of her patience. She shook her head at them in apology.

"Array, beti, I want to be sure he knows what job his future wife has," Auntie insisted.

Future wife? Aneel was getting married? Or at least meeting women with the intent of getting married? Karina stiffened under his touch and felt the blood drain from her face, and her heart quite possibly stopped. She worked to not show any emotion on her face, to make it a mask. She had no idea if she was successful or not.

Aneel cleared his throat, and stroked her back with his thumb, as if trying to explain. But she couldn't move. If she looked at him, she might cry. If she turned and left, she would most certainly cry. Though they had made no promises of any kind to each other. She'd barely let him call her friend. So what was going on inside her, her body...her heart...right now?

She made a beeline for the one place she felt in control. The kitchen. And then, she started talking. Really fast. Very high-pitched. Clearly someone had taken over her mouth.

"Wife? That's fantastic. You know, Aneel and I were going to make these cute mini gulab jamun for a client I cater for, but they would make a great sweet at a wedding. In fact, the pani puri shooters we made last week are a great appetizer.

Oh my god. This is so exciting—I'll totally have to do your menu, if you want, I mean. Of course, you can pick whoever you want to cater your events, it doesn't have to be me, I mean it could be me, but it doesn't have to, I mean I might not even have the time since I could be head chef at Fusion if I manage to win the TV competition thing. Thing."

Toral just stared at her. Tara Auntie was beaming. And Aneel, who she was finally able to look at, was shaking his head.

"Aneel," Toral said softly as she turned in the barstool. "I should go."

Aneel nodded at her. "Yes. It was great meeting you."

"I'll be in touch, beta." Tara Auntie grinned at him, but Toral shot her a glare.

"No." Toral glanced at Karina. "I won't." She squeezed Aneel's hand and whispered something Karina couldn't hear. It didn't matter—Karina was coming up with ways to cut off the hand that Toral had lain on Aneel.

Toral and Tara Auntie left, and then it was just Karina and Aneel. The door clicked, and he turned to her, his face unreadable. He said nothing, simply walked into the small kitchen where she had frozen to the spot.

The kitchen was small enough that with the two of them standing in the middle, there wasn't a lot of room leftover.

He had a bit of scruff on his jaw this morning, like he hadn't had time to shave. He smelled like soap and spices, so he had showered. He was wearing a simple black long-sleeved T-shirt, like he wore under his whites, and jeans.

He rolled up the sleeves of his shirt and started chopping vegetables. Tomato, bell pepper, onion. He glanced at her, definite heat in his eyes.

She could not tear her eyes from his corded forearms and hands that skillfully and quickly chopped everything he touched in less than minutes. He put it all aside, then set his gaze firmly on hers.

She gasped as if he'd touched her. She couldn't move.

He pulled out eggs, cracked them and proceeded to whip them by hand. He looked at her and sighed, then put the eggs aside as well. He moved toward her, his heated gaze so intent on her she could feel it.

He stopped close enough that she had to turn her eyes up to see his face. He scrubbed his face with his hand. "You're going to cater my wedding?" His voice was soft, low, and he gently tucked a stray piece of hair behind her ear.

The touch was light but lingering, and she involuntarily dipped her head into his hand. He drew his fingers down her jaw and to her neck. Her heart pounded, and her skin tingled wherever he touched it.

"Well." She cleared her throat and swallowed. "I'm a good caterer."

He frowned and nodded, stepping yet closer to her. "True." He drew his fingers forward under her chin and lifted her gaze to his, so she could see properly into his eyes.

Her breath caught, not just because of his beauty, which was knee-melting, but because of what she saw in his eyes. She could see clear through to his soul.

He dipped his head closer to her. "I'm not marrying that woman," he whispered.

She swallowed hard. Her heart now thudded rapid-fire as he moved his mouth closer to hers, their breath mingling between them.

"I'm going to kiss you now, is that okay with you, Grumpy?" He quirked a small crooked smile, but his voice was honeyed gravel and reined-in need.

"Mmm-hmm." She nodded and parted her lips. "You're going to have to, or I might lose my mind."

He had the audacity to smirk at her, but she didn't care.

She pressed against him, and he moaned deep in his throat. The sound made her lose all sense of control. She moved to him and lifted her mouth as he gently pressed his lips against hers, tasting, sipping. Her body melted into his, and her mind and heart echoed her surrender to him. *Finally.*

Then, as if he could read her mind, he gently pushed his leg between hers, moved his hand to the back of her head and deepened the kiss. She opened for him, wrapping her arms around his shoulders, pulling him close and taking everything from that kiss that he was willing to give.

Chapter Twenty-Six

She tasted like cinnamon and cardamom, her citrus scent filling him. She felt like home. The look of pain in her eyes, in her body when she saw another woman sitting here talking about being *his*—was unbearable. She, who had suffered so much, who had given so much. For her to think for just one second that he did not return her love—because that was what this was—was unacceptable.

He claimed her with their kiss. He was hers, to do with as she pleased. They parted for air, and he placed one hand on that curvy bottom and in one motion lifted her to the counter. Her lips were swollen and wet, her eyes lidded with desire—for him. She fisted his T-shirt in both hands and pulled him to her with such force, their teeth banged against each other. But she did not pull away as she tasted him thoroughly.

She knew it, too. He was hers.

He bunched the sides of her T-shirt until he could get his hands on her skin. Warm and soft as silk—he'd known it would be. What he hadn't known, what he could never have predicted was how all he wanted was for his every touch to make her happy. He roamed her back and waist with his fingers, all the while his lips never left her mouth. Her soft moans pulling him under.

Then her hands found the edge of his T-shirt, and when she touched his skin, he was scorched by her touch. He kissed her jaw, ran his tongue down her neck, pressing his lips to every inch of her.

His hands eased upward, and his mouth tasted down, ready to meet at the swell of her breasts.

And then she pulled back.

"I... I...can't." She was breathless as she gently pushed his chest. He took a step back as she lowered her shirt. She was dazed, unsatisfied, but a part of her brain remained functional.

He looked as dazed as she felt, his breath coming hard. His oh-so-fine-muscular chest heaved with every breath. Instinct and need had her ready to rip his shirt off and continue down this road, whether it be here in the kitchen or in his bed. Or both.

But some small rational part of her brain that held Veer's face made her collect her breath and her senses.

"I'm sorry. I wanted this. I really did. Or at least I thought I did. I mean I wanted to kiss you..." She paused. "I've wanted to kiss you for a long time."

Aneel was bracing his hands on the adjacent counter as if he needed it to hold him up as he recovered from kissing her. "Then what—"

She shook her head at him. "My life is not about what I want anymore. This is how I ended up with Veer." She paused, and he nodded, still not looking at her. "Chirag and I were dating, and we were young and passionate—"

Aneel snapped his head to her and narrowed his eyes, a low growl emitting from deep within him.

"Right. You don't need the details. Anyway, I gave in to youth and hormones, and the next thing I knew I had husband, then a baby, then an ex-husband. While I love Veer more than life itself, I can't do that again. I can't do that to Veer. It was one thing for Chirag to break a promise to me, but for anyone to hurt Veer—I can't risk it, Aneel. Not for anything."

She hopped down from the counter and continued to gather

herself. She didn't think it was even possible to recover from that kiss, but she was going to have to find a way.

"I would never hurt Veer," Aneel finally said, straightening.

She nodded. She knew that. "I can't risk whatever this..." she waved a hand between them "...might be or might not turn out to be."

"Karina, it was just a kiss—"

"That wasn't just a kiss, and you know it."

"Is that so bad? Let's see where this is going."

"I can't, Aneel. I can't just jump in like that."

"We're not jumping. We can take as long as you like. Veer doesn't have to know that anything has changed between us."

"But if it doesn't work, and you stop coming around? How am I supposed to mend his broken heart?" She shook her head, more determined than ever. "No. This stops here. I'm sorry."

His heart was breaking. Surely, she could hear the pieces crashing to the floor. For that blissful moment, she'd been his. For that blissful moment, he'd had everything he wanted but never dared to dream of.

"Of course," he said. "Don't apologize for looking after Veer. I get it." He tried to sound convincing, because he did believe his words. He simply did not want to. He wanted her and Veer. He already belonged to her. Already loved Veer. He cleared his throat.

She nodded. "I should go."

"I thought we had mini gulab jamun today?" he asked.

"Oh." She waved him off. "You don't have to—I'll just... just go to Rani's."

"But she has no counter space, and her stove is *electric*." They'd been through all this already. It was how they had ended up here in the first place. "And all the ingredients are already here." He sounded pathetic, but if he couldn't have her, he wanted to at least work with her. He'd take any part of her that he could get.

She stared at him, unmoving. He could not read her. He waited. The silence was almost unbearable. "What was with all the chopping and the eggs?"

Heat rushed to his face. He swallowed hard. "I was trying...trying to distract myself from kissing you."

She quirked a smile. "Really?"

"Really." He was that pathetic. "Are we working here, or what?"

"Okay. Fine. But only until my kitchen is fixed. Then you're off the hook. I can manage the catering that I signed up for on my own."

"No deal, Grumpy," he said, a small smile on his face. "The office party in a week is a big payoff. You trying to take the money and run?"

"No. I—I just thought it would be easier—"

"Working that party will not be easier with you doing it alone," he said.

"That's not what I meant."

He met her gaze. "But it is what I meant."

She nodded. "Make those eggs, I'm starving. Then we work."

She moaned as she tasted the eggs, and it sent fire through his body. He was weak. He needed to work. The milk-solids they had made yesterday were in the fridge. He took out the mawa and started to make the smooth dough they would need for the sweet fried balls.

They had to roll the dough into tiny one-centimeter balls before frying them, then add them to hot sugar syrup which was flavored with cardamom and saffron. She started making the balls while Aneel got the syrup ready and the oil heated.

They worked in efficient silence with only the OG Bollywood songs in the background. He did his best not to bump her or touch her in any way, but the kitchen was small, and it was inevitable.

Every touch sent an electric current through his body. It was as if now that he'd touched her, his body wanted more. For her part, aside from being quiet, Karina seemed unbothered by any of it.

They finished, the giant container of mini gulab jamun soaking in sugar syrup, all ready for that office party on Monday.

By the time she was helping him clean up, they'd hardly said a word to each other.

She packed up and walked to the door. "I'll see you at the restaurant in a few."

Then she was gone.

Chapter Twenty-Seven

Karina left Aneel's apartment and kept walking. She had to get home and changed for work tonight. They were going to be on camera, and she had to be in the right frame of mind.

She wanted something she couldn't have. It was nothing new, just part of being a responsible adult.

Pushing him away from her had taken an amount of strength she had not known she possessed. She was only able to do it because her end goal was stability and happiness for Veer.

She sat in her car and indulged herself in a moment and closed her eyes. Big mistake because, of course, that kiss was front and center. She thought of the memory of his mouth on hers, of the electric feeling of his hands on her skin, the gentle promise he'd silently made to her of love and happiness with each caress, each pass of his lips, every stroke of his hands.

She let the tears flow. When she wiped them from her face and started the car, she tucked that memory into her heart, knowing that she would retrieve it time and time again. One day, the memory would not make her cry for what she wanted but would comfort her for what she'd had, even if for only a few minutes.

Aneel focused on the job. On the cooking in which he had always found solace. When his dad left, when his mom died, even as recently as when he and his sister had argued.

The problem was that in this situation, the object of his angst also cooked. He found it challenging to unfold a recipe without remembering a comment she'd made or wondering what her take might be on something new he had considered.

He tried nonetheless. He envied the line cooks. What he needed was to chop things mindlessly and allow his thoughts to fall into place.

Karina had walked out of his apartment, and he had simply stood there, trying to make sense of what had occurred.

Tara Auntie had been threatening him with her niece for over a month. He had been able to dodge the older woman with the chaos of his schedule. But last night she had cornered him at the mailbox. Toral was in town for an interview; she would bring her to his apartment in the morning for chai.

He had sighed and resigned himself to it. Not that he wanted to meet women, but these aunties were not to be ignored. He tried and tried, but every so often, he found himself having chai with a beautiful woman who had no more interest in him than he had in her.

Toral was no different. Though, just prior to Karina's arrival, Toral had mentioned that her dad grew up in Uganda and that the cloves from Uganda were perfect for chai masala. He had been ordering them when Karina knocked.

Instinctively he knew that Karina entering was not going to go well, so he had tried to intercept her. Which somehow made things worse.

The next thing he knew, he was making eggs, trying not to kiss her—he was never telling Tyler that, he'd never live it down—and then he was melted into her, and it was everything and nothing like he'd expected.

Karina was right. It wasn't any regular kiss. It was more. He'd slept with women and had less intimacy than that kiss with Karina.

Because he had not kissed her with only his mouth and lips and hands. He had kissed her with his heart.

As had she, which was why she'd run from it. He loved Karina; he had probably fallen for her seven years ago. Certainly, the few women he'd dated since then hadn't compared to her in any way.

He would wait for her, however long it took. Even if Veer had to be in college before she allowed herself to be happy. Aneel didn't have much choice. It was Karina or no one.

He finished the evening and found her in the locker room. "Trying to sneak out, Grumpy?"

"You don't need to use the nickname," she said softly as they walked out to the parking lot together.

"But I like it," he insisted. "And it fits."

She gave him a scalding look, and it settled him. At least she was trying to act normal. "I just wanted to check with you—"

"About tomorrow morning?"

She nodded as they reached her car. "We need to work on the party. I'll be over at 8:00 a.m."

"Right. See you then." He stepped back as she got in her car. He watched her drive off as he got in his own.

Morning rolled around sooner than he was ready for it after a night of tossing and turning. The only thing he could think about was Karina's mouth on his, her hands on his skin, how her body felt flush against his. It was more than lust. He'd seen it in her eyes, felt it in her kiss.

She had said so herself. *It was more than just a kiss.*

Karina showed up at 8:00 a.m. sharp, as promised. Her hair was in a messy bun, and she had on leggings and an oversize T-shirt. There were dark circles under her eyes, and she was sipping on a gigantic Yeti of coffee.

"Hey," she said, entering.

"Hey. You look like how I feel," he said.

She nodded. "Shall we?"

"Sure. Saira is still here. She's getting ready for school."

Karina stiffened.

"What?"

"I don't think she likes me very much," Karina whispered.

"She doesn't really know you," he told her.

"When does she leave?"

"An hour."

Karina grinned. "Perfect. Move over and give me a few minutes."

Aneel stepped aside. Anything that put a smile on Karina's face. She looked around his whole kitchen, muttering to herself, until finally she started mixing and blending. Delicious aromas emitted from his kitchen within twenty minutes.

Saira walked out. "Bhaiya. Whatever you're making, it smells amazing."

"It's not me." He pointed to Karina in the kitchen.

Karina gave her a wide smile. "I thought I'd make breakfast for you both for letting me use the kitchen." She plated French toast for all three of them.

"I don't...usually...eat breakfast." But Saira sidled up to the breakfast bar and picked up a fork. "But I suppose I could give this a try." She put a bite in her mouth and groaned. "Bhaiya. Learn this from her." She looked at Karina, a smile on her mouth. "This is fantastic. I'm sorry for all the things I said about you."

"You haven't said anything—"

"Not out loud, I haven't. But I was wrong. Anyone who can make French toast like this..." She did a chef's kiss. "Thank you." She ate her French toast and half of Aneel's before she ran out the door for school.

No sooner had the door shut than Karina looked at Aneel, victory in her eyes. "Now, she knows me."

* * *

Saira was back before Aneel left for the restaurant. Karina had left a couple hours earlier, their work for the party done. He had thoroughly enjoyed himself with her, just cooking side by side, bumping into each other in the cramped space. It had still taken every ounce of self-control to not pull her in and kiss her senseless.

Saira was very chatty, but Aneel found it hard to focus on what she was saying.

"Want to come see it before I finalize?"

"Yeah, sure." He was looking for his whites. He had pressed them himself and put them in his closet...

"It's a five-bedroom house in New Jersey."

"Sounds good," he said, scouring his small closet. Not there.

"It'll be great for my baby. Seeing as how I'm pregnant."

"Okay. Just let me know when to meet you." Maybe Saira's closet?

"Bhaiya. Are you even listening?" She had followed him to her room.

"What?" Not there, either. He turned to leave the room.

"What's the matter with you?" She grabbed him by his biceps. "I just told you I was pregnant and moving to Jersey, and you said okay."

"You're *pregnant*?" His heart fell into his stomach.

"No. You idiot. I'm just trying to get your attention. You've been a weirdo all week."

"So you thought you'd give me a heart attack?"

"Bhaiya. What. Is. Going. On?"

"Hey! Anybody home?" Tyler walked in. "What's going on? Why are we hanging out in Saira's room?"

"Your friend is acting all weird, that's what."

"I'm fine." Aneel glared at Saira. "I just can't find my whites, and I have to get to work."

Tyler thumbed toward the living room. "I think they're hanging on the hook by the door?"

Aneel's eyes widened. "Seriously?" He pushed past Tyler and his sister.

"This has something to do with Karina Mistry, doesn't it?" Saira said.

"No," Aneel said, maybe more forcefully than necessary.

Tyler and Saira exchanged a glance.

Whatever.

"So, it's definitely her," Tyler said. "Spill it." He glanced at his watch. "You have six minutes before I have to leave for a meeting, and I'm dropping Saira at the doggie hospital."

Saira rolled her eyes. "Can you not call it that?"

"It's apt," Tyler insisted.

Aneel glared at them. "It doesn't matter. She's not interested."

"Well, that's not true," Saira said. "She literally made me breakfast this morning—the *best* French toast I have ever had, by the way—because Bhaiya told her the reason I didn't like her was because I didn't know her." She shrugged at her brother. "The walls are thin."

"What?" Tyler asked. "Can you tell her I don't like her, either? Maybe she'll cook for me."

"*I* cook for you, Tyler. Like all the time." Aneel stared at him in disbelief.

"Well, yeah." Tyler shrugged one shoulder. "But I want to try the French toast."

Saira turned her back to Tyler and faced Aneel. "If she's cooking for me, she likes you."

"That may be, but she's not... She doesn't want to risk her son getting too close if things don't work out."

Tyler and Saira went silent.

"Say something," he demanded.

"She's not wrong," Tyler said.

Saira said nothing.

Aneel shook his head. "I should go, and you'll be late."

"She wants a guarantee that if she and her son fall for you, you won't leave," Saira said.

"Basically."

"So, give it to her."

Chapter Twenty-Eight

Tomorrow was the last challenge as well as the fancy office party Karina and Aneel had been working on. Her whole family as well as Aneel had stayed up late last night finishing up, so she could organize and be ready for the party. She hardly even noted that the last competition would take place the morning of the party.

She slept a bit late, as did her whole house. It was still quiet when she woke and made her morning coffee. It was rare that she had these quiet moments to herself, so she curled up on the sofa with a warm blanket and sipped her life-giving coffee.

The blanket was the one Aneel had used when they'd watched that movie with Veer. It still smelled like him. A glutton for punishment, Karina wrapped it tighter around herself and inhaled deeply. She wished she had her mom to talk to. Maybe if she'd had her mom when she dated Chirag, she wouldn't even be in this situation.

Which situation would that be? her mother would ask.

The one where I kissed a man I really like and have feelings for, but I pushed him away because I have to look out for Veer.

The sofa dipped on either side of her, and her sisters bookended her, each a bit groggy but holding a mug of coffee. She looked at them but didn't share the blanket. They rolled their eyes and each got their own.

"Don't you have a hot husband in your bed, Rani?" Karina asked.

Rani flushed. "I do. But we haven't had sister time in a while." She grinned and sipped her coffee.

Karina looked at Sona.

"You've been really weird for the past few days, so I called her over for a sister intervention." Sona yawned into her coffee mug.

"Weird? How?"

"Were you just now having a conversation with our mother?" Sona asked.

Karina nodded.

"You've been quiet, and you randomly smile or stare into space. And then you look really sad. And when Aneel is over, you guys are completely weird with each other. The tension between you two last night was taut."

"She slept with him," Rani said.

"I did not sleep with him," Karina countered.

Her sisters stared at her.

"I *didn't*. I just kissed him."

Her sisters shared a look and a smile.

"Is he a bad kisser? Because that can be taught, you know," Rani said.

Karina eyed her sister. "No. He's a pretty excellent kisser." She sighed at the memory.

Rani narrowed her eyes at her. "You have feelings. Like real feelings for him."

Karina sipped her coffee and did not make eye contact.

Sona turned to face her. "It's Veer, isn't it?" She looked at Rani for confirmation.

"You have feelings for Aneel, but you're afraid because of Veer," Rani said.

Karina nodded.

"Aneel loves Veer," Sona said. "And your kiddo absolutely adores him. Have you seen them together?"

"I can't risk it," Karina said. "What if I date Aneel, and it doesn't work out? Where does that leave Veer?"

"But what if you date Aneel, and it does work out?" Sona asked.

"It's not a risk I'm willing to take." Karina sipped her coffee. "I'm not going through all that again."

"Going through what? You pregnant again?" Sona smirked.

Karina rolled her eyes. "Of course not." She pursed her lips at her sister. "Aneel's a great kisser, but he's not *that* great."

This earned her laughter from her sisters.

"What did Mom say just now?" Rani asked.

Tears welled in Karina's eyes. "Nothing. But you two showed up."

Her sisters each put an arm around her and she did the same, hugging them tight. "I just want to be a good mom, like she was. She always put us first," Karina said.

"You *are* a great mom," Sona said.

"Look how great Veer is," Rani said. "That's because of you."

Karina allowed her sisters' words to fill her up. "You two are the best. Don't think I don't know how much you all love Veer, too. You're in there, too. I couldn't do this without you, and Papa."

"You don't have to," Sona said.

Karina let herself sink into her sisters' love for a while. They sipped their coffees slowly and left the sofa to bring over muffins to munch on.

"What's up with Papa and this Rupa woman?" Karina asked her sisters.

"They are adorable," Sona said.

"Papa is *finally* letting himself be happy again," Rani said with a pointed look at Karina.

Veer finally woke, joining them on the sofa. Karina put the final touches on the food.

In the late afternoon, there was a knock at the mudroom door. Her sisters turned to her as Veer jumped off the sofa. "Aneel Uncle is here! I knew he would come."

Karina shook her head. "I don't think so." Aneel hadn't mentioned it. And she hadn't bothered to remind him.

Veer raced to open the door, Karina behind him. She hadn't even showered today, as if not showering would protect her when he didn't show.

She opened the door and sure enough, Aneel was there, a bag of food in his hands, looking absolutely kissable in his leather jacket and what she now knew were his comfy jeans. His hair was damp from a shower. Lucky the fall had given way to a false spring for a day, so it wasn't even nippy.

She stepped aside to let him in.

"I told you, Mommy!"

"Yes, you did," she said, taking in Aneel though she had just seen him last night. "Did we forget something?"

Aneel looked at her. "Movie night."

Veer was nodding his head. "Movie night, Mom. We're watching *Iron Man*. Remember? I'll get it set up."

Last weekend was a lifetime ago, when they had sat in the fort and had pizza, just the three of them. It had been comfortable, cozy, right.

She nodded. "Sorry, it slipped my mind."

"Jeez, Grumpy. Next time write it down," Aneel said with a hint of a smirk as he passed her and went to the kitchen. Like he belonged there.

"Whatever, Sunshine." She side-eyed him. "What's in the bag?"

He grinned at her as he put the bag on the island and started removing items.

Karina could barely hold in her laughter. "Frozen Tater

Tots. Chocolate cake from a grocery store." She wrinkled her nose. "And McDonald's hamburgers."

Her sisters came to the kitchen and took in the food. Aneel had already found a cookie sheet and covered it with foil and was unceremoniously dumping the Tater Tots on to it.

"I thought you were a chef," Rani said to him.

"I am." Aneel popped the Tater Tots into the oven. Her oven. "But sometimes Veer asks for food that isn't made by a chef." He shrugged. "He wants regular junk food." He met Karina's eyes and held her gaze, as if he wasn't afraid. As if all he wanted was chance to love her. To love Veer.

"It's okay, Aneel," Sona whispered. "We know about the make-out session."

He flushed as deep a red as anyone with brown skin could, and Karina thought she would like to fall through the floor. She glared at her sisters.

"Go get wine, Sona," she grumbled.

Sona left with a smile.

"Are you ready, Aneel Uncle?" Veer called from the family room. "Because I'm going to show you—" He sniffed the air. "Tater Tots?" He ran back to the kitchen. "McDonald's?" He hugged Aneel's legs. "You're the best. I was afraid Mom was going to make something 'special.'" He rolled his eyes.

Karina gaped at him. "Hey!"

"Come on, Veer, let's go get Param Mama and Dada for the movie." Rani took Veer's hand and shot Karina a look before she left with her son.

"Well, your sisters are not subtle," Aneel said.

"Did you think they would be?"

"No." He took the time to look at her. "You look gorgeous."

"I haven't even showered today."

"Is that what that smell is?" He wrinkled his nose and chuckled. "It doesn't matter," his voice intimate. "You're always beautiful."

She melted a bit where she stood. "Don't."

He shook his head. "I will. I will tell you how beautiful you are and what a great mom you are and how that kiss was anything but just a kiss, and all I can think about is doing it again." He slowly moved closer to her as he spoke.

"You came," she said. "For movie night."

"Of course." He smiled at her. "I promised Veer. I didn't forget like some people."

"I didn't forget." She looked at him.

"You didn't forget to shower, did you?" he asked softly, close enough that she could envelope herself in his soap and spice scent.

She shook her head. "I thought if I showered, it meant I was looking forward to you coming over. And I didn't want to expect you and then be disappointed that you didn't show."

He showed her that crooked smile she loved so much. "And now?"

"You came for Veer." Tears burned behind her eyes. "Even when I said I didn't want to be with you. I kind of wish I'd showered."

He moved closer to her, his breath mingling with hers. "Give us a chance. We won't involve Veer any further than we have, I promise. No holding hands in front of him. Nothing that makes him think we are anything but colleagues or friends. Give *us* a chance and see how great we can be." He paused, and she looked up at him. "Please."

This man was literally begging her for a chance, and all she wanted to do was give it. She bit her bottom lip. She deserved a bit of happiness, didn't she? Wasn't that what her sisters had spent the day telling her. Hell, even her seventy-year-old dad was dating. "We have to go slow."

"Turtles will outpace us." He grinned, not bothering to hide the hope in his eyes.

She laughed, hearing her own nervousness fading.

"I don't care, as long we do it together." Seriously, his voice was a balm to her nerves. And his words were true.

Joy, the likes of which she only felt from Veer, entered her heart, and a giggle escaped her. "Yes. Okay. Yes."

Aneel's faced lit up like the sun, those two dimples were freed, and she thought she'd melt right there. She leaned in to kiss him.

He pulled back. "Uh, uh, uh. Not in front of the kid."

"Aneel Uncle!" Veer called from the family room.

"Just getting the Tater Tots," Aneel called out before leaning toward her again. "Besides, you need a shower." He dodged her smack as he grabbed the McDonald's. "Who wants a burger?" he called, still grinning like a fool at her as he walked to the family room.

Chapter Twenty-Nine

By the time Aneel got to the restaurant the next day, Karina was in her whites and waiting for the competition to be announced. This was the last Monday competition. He didn't care what she said. She was beautiful no matter what she wore.

The camera crew was waiting as he made it to the kitchen still buttoning his whites.

Deepak stood up. "Today is our last competition. By the end of this week, we will have a new head chef." He looked around. "Today's competition is small plates."

Aneel glanced over at Karina. It took a tremendous amount of self-control to not go over and kiss her. She met his gaze, and whatever she saw, made her gape and flush. She turned to her staff. But not before she ran her eyes over him from head to toe. His whole body heated.

"Okay, chefs. Begin," Deepak said with a flourish.

"So small plates are Chef Mistry's finest hour." Aneel started the banter. "What are you going to put on those plates today, Chef?" He avoided looking too closely her way, lest the camera pick up on the new and delicious tension between them.

"As if I'd tell you, Chef Rawal." Karina grinned like she did every week. Well maybe not the exact same way. There appeared to be an extra bounce in her step. Some heat in her gaze. In his as well.

Aneel nodded and forced his camera smile at her. "Bring it on, Chef."

They had to make three different dishes. Aneel made traditional chaat, dabeli sandwich, spicy and sweet—like it was from a cart in Delhi—and batter-dipped chili pakora.

"Time," Deepak called and both of them presented.

Karina had made Tater Tot chaat, pav bhaji with soy crumble, and spinach and kale pakora.

Aneel's jaw dropped. "Chef Mistry used Tater Tots?"

"Chef Rawal *didn't* use Tater Tots, and did traditional dishes?" she mock-gasped.

"I can be taught, Chef," he said with a small smirk and heat in his eyes. He particularly loved the flush in her cheeks when she saw that.

"Good to know, Chef," she said softly, her own eyes nearly smoldering.

The judges tasted and asked questions and took their time deliberating. Divya Shah tasted but did not comment as she watched them. Her gaze shifting from one chef to another, a small smile sat on her face.

Amar Virani approached, wearing an Iron Man T-shirt under his open whites. "It was close this week. I mean, these two are extremely talented in all they do, but this week was exceptionally close. However, the Tater Tots and the soy crumble did it for me." He turned to Karina. "Chef Mistry, enjoy your week as head chef."

Karina blanched. She'd had no expectation of winning this week. In fact, she had almost planned on not being the head this week. She had a party next weekend, not to mention the big wedding in less than two weeks. How was she supposed to pull that off and run the kitchen?

Aneel came over and offered his hand. His grip was firm, and she noticed, not for the first time, the calluses on his skin.

She let her hand linger longer than necessary. "Congrats, Chef Mistry. You'll be great."

"Yeah." She nodded, still working out the logistics in her head as Aneel slowly withdrew his hand.

"Act excited," he murmured, leaning in to her. He tilted his head slightly toward the camera on them.

She snapped out of it. "Better take notes, Chef Rawal. So you'll know what I like from my sous chef."

He nodded and chuckled for the camera, but concern shone in his eyes.

"Cut," called Rakesh. "Let's clean up."

Karina relaxed her shoulders and started cleaning up.

"Everything okay?" Aneel asked quietly.

"I'll be fine. Just that I have the catering events." She shrugged. "I'll figure it out."

Aneel furrowed his brow. "Happy to help as always."

She grinned as she met his eyes and leaned in to whisper, "I was hoping you would say that." She itched to touch him.

"Karina," he asked slowly. "Do you even need the position anymore?"

She glanced at him as she continued to clean. "Of course I do."

He shrugged. "I'm just saying, you're a very talented caterer. And you always look so happy when we're working together. Catering has a huge kitchen—"

"I don't want to be a caterer. I need to be head chef," Karina told him.

But did she? She was making some very good money these past few weeks from catering. And she was only running around because she was trying to do both. If she only catered, she might be around more to pick up and drop off Veer, spend time with him. It had been a pleasure the few times she could put off cooking until after she and Veer had had some time together. She glanced up and found Aneel watching her.

"Just something to think about," he said.

She nodded.

The cleanup done, she and Aneel changed out of their whites and walked out together. He accompanied her to her car as he always did. She leaned against the car and looked up at him. "This sneaking around is going to be a challenge."

"The rules are the rules," he said as he stepped closer to her.

She looked up at him. "I suppose they are."

He moved closer.

"Though the cameras are off. And Veer isn't here." She stood, and their bodies grazed each other. Even that slight touch had her lightheaded.

"True." His eyes darkened, lids hooded while he waited for her. He wouldn't kiss her if she didn't want him to. She was in the driver's seat as long she needed to be. It only deepened her affection for him.

She leaned toward him and brushed her lips on his.

That was all he needed, and he kissed her with as much abandon as he could while standing in a parking lot. His hands cupped her face as if she were a precious gem, but the way he kissed her, he claimed her as his, and she claimed him back.

They parted for breath as the judges passed by.

"About time," Divya called out. "I've been waiting for you two to figure that out all month." She grinned as she grabbed her husband's hand, leaning her head against his shoulder and they walked to their car.

Karina flushed and laughed, falling into Aneel's arms as he laughed and held her. He looked down at her, pure joy in those velvet brown eyes. "Only took us seven years, huh?"

"What?"

"I've been wanting to kiss you since we first met at that competition," Aneel confessed.

"Well, as long as we're confessing." Karina met his eyes.

"I had fully intended to ask you out after the competition."
She paused. "But then I was so angry."

"I'll meet you at your house with the van for the office
party." Aneel took her lip into his mouth. "Unless you want
to come to my place—"

Karina deepened their kiss before pulling back. "Tempting. But I need to get ready for that party."

He mock groaned. "See? A great caterer," he said as she
got into her car.

"I'll be at your house with the van in two hours."

Aneel was right on time, and they easily loaded up the van,
but not before he cornered her in the mudroom for another
make-out session. It took Karina a few minutes to shake off
the dazed feeling, but she wasn't complaining.

She touched up her lipstick and grabbed her clean whites
and hopped in the van next to Aneel.

She was quiet as she contemplated what Aneel had said
about her being a caterer.

"I do love catering," she said as they drove to the office
building.

"So Catering has a huge kitchen—"

"I mean, I like catering from home." She turned to him. "I
suppose I could use a larger kitchen in the future, but right
now, my kitchen is great."

"True." He looked at her.

"I made great money these past few weeks, and I have like
five emails asking for more events." She waved her phone at
him.

"You light up when you talk about it," he said. "You always
have." He grinned at her as he parked the van.

They started unloading just as a woman came out to meet
them.

"Hi. I'm Karina Mistry. I'm the caterer for the party," Karina introduced herself.

"I'm Payal." The woman wore a gorgeous skirt suit that complemented her thin body. Her dark hair was in a low bun, her makeup polished and professional. She greeted them with a lovely smile. "We've been emailing. Right this way."

Karina and Aneel followed Payal through the office area. The office was modern with glass walls and streamlined decor.

"Law offices, right?" Karina asked.

"Correct." Payal opened the door to a beautiful space that had the tables Karina had requested. A small kitchen was also available, which would make reheating easier. "This is our usual party space. My boss, Mr. Mehta will be with you shortly. Please use whatever you need."

"No rush. We need to set up," Karina said.

Aneel got to work warming the hors d'oeuvres, while she began to set up the food stands.

"Karina." A low, deep, *familiar* voice called her name.

Karina froze at the sound. It couldn't be.

But Payal had just said *Mr. Mehta.*

She spun around, and sure enough, Chirag Mehta stood before her. She recognized his face, of course, not to mention that she looked at a miniature version of it every day. But the rest of him did not match the memory of the man who had left her, pregnant with his child.

This Chirag had on an expensive suit, which he filled nicely. He had a calm confidence about him that the Chirag she had known had not possessed.

"Chirag? What...what?" She looked around. *Mr. Mehta.* "Do you *work* here?"

She noted from the corner of her eye that while Aneel was still working, his jaw was clenched, his shoulders had gone rock solid, and his gaze never left her.

Chirag smiled. Had he always been this handsome? "Well, it's my practice, so yes. I suppose."

Chirag had gone to law school to appease his parents, but

he had always told Karina that he had no love of the law. He had passed the bar, but he simply refused to practice. When she met him, he'd been doing odd jobs, and she was doing scut work at Fusion while going to culinary school. He was so care-free, going against what was expected—and she couldn't do that. Her mother had passed a few years prior, her father was finally coming back to life, her sisters were in college, but she herself was still in culinary school, working to pay what her loan would not cover. She was still making dinners and doing laundry and making sure everybody was okay.

Chirag had offered excitement and passion. When the preg-nancy test came back positive, and he suggested that they get married in Vegas, she had agreed. It was the complete oppo-site of anything she would have normally ever done, but that was the reason she did it.

It was only when she had noted the betrayal and hurt on her father's face that she questioned her actions. He would have liked to have been there for his daughter's wedding, no matter the circumstances. She and Chirag got a place of their own, but five months after being married, one month before Veer was born, Chirag left, saying he was overwhelmed and needed to figure out who he was.

Tail between her legs, Karina had moved back in with her father and sisters. She sent word to Chirag that Veer had been born. When she received no response, Karina moved on with her life. The only people who mattered were Veer, her father and her sisters, and of course Param and his family.

But now, here was Chirag, standing in front of her wear-ing a fancy suit in an equally fancy office, telling her he did corporate law. Where was the guy with the beard and ponytail and the eff-you attitude who'd left to find himself?

"What is happening right now?" she asked. "Is there even a party?"

Aneel quietly walked up behind her. She felt his warmth

behind her in the gentle placement of his hand at her lower back. Her heart raced, and her emotions ranged from volcanic anger to severe confusion and deep curiosity from second to second. She leaned into Aneel's touch, the warmth and support grounding her. Not to mention the confirmation that he was hers and he had her back, in every way.

Chirag smiled at her, and she had to blink because that was Veer's smile. "There is a party. I did in fact open this office a year ago—"

Karina's eyes widened, and her mouth dropped open. "You have been in Baltimore for a year?" It had taken them twenty-five minutes to get here from her house. He had been twenty-five minutes away from his son, and he only now contacted her?

"Yes. I was dying to see you, to see our son, but I knew that after everything I had done, you wouldn't want to see me. I couldn't show up empty-handed. I didn't want to show up in my son's life, or yours, without proof that I was a different man than the one who shamefully took off all those years ago."

"You have been gone for four years. I—I—don't even know what to say. You never even responded when I told you Veer was born."

"I was a different man then. A boy. That I walked away from you and Veer will always be my biggest regret. I was too ashamed to even acknowledge him when you told me he was born. To say that I am sorry is barely the tip of the apology that I owe you both." Chirag paused. "I wanted to meet with you, so you could see for yourself the person I am now. The boy you knew is...gone."

Karina was furious. "You tricked me...you let me think this was Payal's business." Or had he? Payal had said she was the office manager. Her breath was coming hard, and the words were just falling out of her mouth. "A year, Chirag? A year!" She was shouting now.

"When I finally got my head together, I—I wanted to *be* somebody before I met my son. Before I saw *you* again. I was so ashamed of what I had done, I couldn't show up with nothing but promises that you would never trust I could keep."

"Breathe," Aneel whispered just loud enough for her to hear.

She inhaled and exhaled as she gaped at Chirag.

"Please. Just hear me out," Chirag was begging.

She studied him. He had reached out for the last month via email, and she had ignored him. So he had hired her to cater. She really had no desire to be in this room with him. But damn, he looked just like Veer. Veer's voice echoed in her head, all his questions about family, his dad... Maybe she should at least hear him out. She turned her head slightly toward Aneel. "Can you—?"

He nodded. "I can step out and call your sister and make sure Veer knows you'll be extra late." His hand still pressed gently against her back, but his eyes were hard as he looked at Chirag. "Then I'll be back."

"Actually, Aneel." She turned to him. "I need to have this conversation on my own."

"Of course," he replied, a small smile on his face.

She turned her focus back to Chirag. "Fine. We'll finish here, and then we can talk."

Chirag's face lit up. "Thank you, Karina. It's more than I deserve, and I appreciate it."

Karina rested a hard gaze on this "new" Chirag. She kept her voice cold. "Don't get too excited."

Chapter Thirty

The end of the night came both too fast and too slow. Before she knew it, the van was packed up once again.

"You okay?" Aneel asked as he got into the van.

She nodded. "I'll be okay. Just tell Sona what's up."

"I can stay, if you want." Aneel nodded in Chirag's direction with a look on his face she didn't think she'd ever seen before. Anger and something else. Sadness. Fear.

"Thanks. But just let my sister know."

Aneel was on his way to her house to be with Veer. It was really the only reason she was able to go with this new Chirag to the bar.

She didn't want to go home and change. She simply unbuttoned her chef's whites as they walked to the bar next door.

She ordered an old fashioned.

He raised an eyebrow at her. "What happened to Sauvignon blanc?"

"You aren't the only one who changed, Chirag," she snipped at him.

"I suppose that's true," he said. He looked at the bartender. "Make that two old fashioneds. And go ahead and make it Bulleit for both."

"I'll have Woodford Reserve," she told the bartender and smirked at Chirag.

He raised his eyebrows, and she simply looked away. She didn't want to be here.

"Let's get to it, Chirag. Did you hire me just so you could talk?" Karina didn't bother trying to keep her anger from her voice.

"I am sorry for doing that. It was my last resort after all my emails went unanswered. I hestitated, even considered just coming to the house—"

Karina stiffened.

"But I didn't want to surprise you with Veer there—the whole thing is a mess that I know I created, and I am sorry."

Karina simply nodded, her jaw still tight, eyes trying to burn a hole through Chirag. The feared and unspoken question hung in the air. *What do you want?*

Chirag looked at her. And she saw a remnant of the man that she had known. "I told you that I was going to find myself." He said softly. "And I did. In Nepal."

It was her turn to raise an eyebrow.

"You're going to have to be more specific than that."

"When I first got there, it was all meditation and yoga, which was freeing and focusing all at once. Six months in, I met some people, lawyers in fact. They were on retreat. I spoke with them while they refilled their wells. They loved the law, and they loved their jobs. They just needed a break every so often. The more I talked to them, the more I realized that I did in fact like the law. That I had enjoyed law school. I just hadn't been in the right place to see it, I was so caught up in the idea of rebellion." He paused and looked at her.

Karina studied him. Chirag was many things. Irresponsible. Spontaneous. Charming. Selfish. Annoying, even. But he was not a liar. She saw no mistruth in him whatsoever. He was telling her the truth. He was baring his soul, such as it was.

"So let me get this straight," she said. "You were rebellious, and you said you hated law school. You passed the bar with flying colors. You went to Nepal, and you realized that, hey, you actually like being a lawyer?"

"People usually come back from such an experience more spiritual or having found peace." He sighed. "I found that as well. I was drifting when we were together." He spun his glass around, studying it for a bit before turning back to her. "When we found out we were pregnant, and then we got married—" he held up a hand "—I know that marriage was my idea. But as we got closer to the birth, I got scared. I didn't know what to do. I wanted to do the right thing, I just didn't know what that was."

"*You* were scared? *You* thought you didn't know what to do?" She elevated her voice, not really caring who heard at this point. "*I* was scared. I had no idea what I was doing. I was lost and confused. And then *you left*. Did you think that would make it better?" Karina was at a loss for words. She couldn't believe that he was saying these things to her. She had been just as scared as he was, but she couldn't run.

"I don't know what I was thinking," Chirag confessed, his voice softening as hers got harder. "I'm so sorry, it was so very wrong of me. I think I thought you had your family and that you would be okay. Honestly, I probably wasn't thinking about you at all."

"You think?" Karina snapped at him. "Because I was alone. I had my family, but in the end, this was my child." She paused. "I've had to raise him on my own. He asks me about dads all the time. Specifically, where is his dad. Or can he have a dad. Can I get him a dad. What am I supposed to say? How do I explain all this to him?"

"That's why I waited a whole year until I was stable, so that I had something to offer you, something to offer Veer. I want to meet him, Karina. I want to make this right. Please let me make this right."

"You can't make this right. You can't make up for the past four and a half years that you haven't been here. I was pregnant when you left. I delivered him on my own. I took care of him on my own. Thank God my father and my sisters were there to help me, to watch him while I went to school and worked."

"You don't have to do that anymore. I'm financially stable now." His voice softened. "Let me meet him. Let me make this up to you."

"You can't just throw money at it, Chirag, and hope that it gets better."

"I'm not here to just throw money at it. If you'll give me a chance, I want to be part of my son's life. He should know who his father is." He paused and looked at her. "I'm ready to be part of your life. To be the man I should have been four and half years ago. I'm so sorry that I wasn't, but I am now. Is it really too late?" His voice softened, and the earnestness came through. "I know that I made a huge mistake in leaving you pregnant and alone. I was a different person." He spoke slowly and earnestly. "I didn't deserve you. I didn't deserve our son. I'm not that man anymore."

Karina was angry, and she had every goddamn right to be. "Do you think you deserve us now?" She scowled at him. "Because you've made some money and had a realization that you walked away from a responsibility? And now you feel bad about it and want to ease your conscience?" She stood. "No, thank you."

"I love you."

She froze.

"I have always loved you. That never changed. All this time."

She narrowed her eyes at him. "You don't love me."

"I never stopped loving you. I truly am begging you for a second chance. I've made something of myself. For the sole reason of being a better man for you and our son."

Karina just stared at him. She didn't want to believe him. She wanted to rail at him. She wanted to be angry and self-righteous, as she knew she had a right to be. Chirag was not a liar. He believed what he was saying. He believed that he loved her.

"I know it's a risk and a long shot, but what if we could be a family?" he asked. His shoulders drooped as he held her gaze with those oh-so-familiar-eyes. The picture he had painted with the expensive suit and the fancy office and the money clearly at his disposal fell away as Chirag bared his soul to her. "I want that more than anything. Is that so bad?"

Aneel had never wanted to punch someone as badly as he wanted to punch Chirag Mehta. He had clearly not wanted to do anything with Karina or his son four years ago, so where did he get off tricking her into meeting now?

Aneel had watched Karina all evening. Her focus was clearly on what this would mean for her son. It had killed him to leave her, but he knew she needed to know that her son was safe. And he respected her need to have this conversation on her own.

No matter that he was torn up inside.

Aneel was pretending to watch a movie, Sona and Rani pretending beside him, when Karina came barging in through the mudroom door. Of course he had told her sisters they'd met Chirag. He and her sisters sat up and looked at each other. Veer had long since been put to bed.

If Karina was startled or shocked to see him there, she didn't say anything. She simply pulled out a bottle of wine and four glasses and poured generously. Sona grabbed Aneel by the elbow and they all went to the island to claim their glasses. Still no one spoke. Karina gulped down half her glass before she opened her mouth.

"He's an idiot. He's a complete idiot." She paced the kitchen. "This is ridiculous. He can't just show up here after four and a half years and decide that he wants to be part of my son's life, that he wants to be a part of my life."

Aneel's heart stopped.

"That's ridiculous. He can't do that," Rani railed.

Aneel remained quiet but was inclined to agree. Was Karina seriously considering doing this? Chirag had walked out on them. He had no right to come back and demand to see Veer.

"He gave up his chance," Rani continued. "Tell Chirag to go eff off and you're done with him."

Aneel would be happy to punch him as well.

Sona turned to her sisters. "He's Veer's father. Veer has a right to know who his dad is."

"Maybe, but when he's older, and he can handle it. Not now. He's four." Rani was fuming.

Karina chugged the rest of her glass of wine and poured another. Her gaze darted between her sisters, landing softly on him. Something in her eyes unsettled him.

"He's already asking about his dad," Karina said. "He asks Papa. He asks Sona. He asks Param. He wants to know where his dad is and why he doesn't have one."

"But you would be exposing him, opening him up to pain and hurt if this guy decides he wants to leave again. A good dad would have stuck around and made it work. This guy abandoned you, abandoned him, Karina. How could you even possibly consider this?" Rani continued.

Aneel knew he liked Rani.

"I have to consider this. You don't think I want to tell Chirag to get the hell out of town and leave us be? To spare my son the pain of a father who may not live up to his expectations?" Karina was pacing again. She took a swig from her glass. "But this is not just about me. I have to think about Veer and what he might want. What if Chirag turns out to be a great father and Veer is happy? I can't discount that."

"His track record isn't good," Rani snapped.

Karina narrowed her eyes. "His track record is he left. He

is now saying he has changed. Maybe he has. I might owe it to him as Veer's father to let him meet Veer." She paused.

"She has a point," Sona said. "Chirag is Veer's father. Veer is asking about his dad." She shrugged. "It could go either way."

Aneel had remained silent through all of this. This was Karina's decision. Of course he had an opinion, but he was biased.

Karina looked at him. "You're facing something similar."

Aneel shook his head. "No. My dad was...not well. He's back, but I'm a grown adult. It's not the same."

"Both dads want to see their sons, make things right," Karina said.

"I've had twenty years to be angry. Veer doesn't have that," Aneel answered.

Karina nodded, her gaze still on him.

He narrowed his eyes. There was something else. She was...holding back.

Realization hit him in the gut. The ground beneath him slipped away, and all the oxygen in the room seemed to be gone. He was lightheaded and heavy all at the same time. It was a wonder he was still standing.

"He's still in love with you." Aneel's voice was not much more than a low growl.

Karina froze. "How did you...?"

Aneel softened his gaze at her. "Why wouldn't he be?"

"Are you serious?" Rani fired up again.

Karina nodded, but her gaze never left Aneel's.

He clenched his jaw. He couldn't even think about the next question. Did she still love Chirag? "What did you say to him?"

She shook her head. "I was in shock."

"Did you tell him about us?" Aneel asked.

"*Us* just started a few days ago. What was I supposed to say?" She flailed her arms but did not meet his eyes.

Bull. There had been something between them for much longer than that. "That there was someone else."

"I told him I would consider letting him see Veer."

He needed to get out of there. He opened his mouth to say as much, but nothing came out. He simply turned and walked out.

Chapter Thirty-One

"Are you in love with Chirag?" Sona asked after Aneel had left. When had Sona become the rational sister?

"No? I don't know," Karina said, still staring at the space emptied when Aneel had stalked out. "I honestly have not thought about my feelings. This whole time. It's all always been about Veer." Anger filled her again. "He thinks he can just swoop in here after four years just because he's making a ton of money now, and I'm supposed to let him see my son? I'm supposed to let him be a part of my son's life?" She downed the rest of her wine and went to pour another glass.

"But I don't know. Maybe I should let him see his son. A child needs a father. And Veer keeps asking about his. How long am I supposed to put him off? Maybe he can meet Chirag. If Chirag turns out to be a jerk… Well, then Veer will know that people don't always turn out to be who we expect them to be. And that'll be that. Veer will be hurt, and that will suck, but he will have answers. And then we'll be done."

"He's only four," Rani insisted.

"But he should know," Sona told her. "Think about what Aneel said."

Karina snapped her gaze to Sona.

"He had twenty years to hate his father. Veer could go down that road. Or what if years from now he finds out that Chirag wanted to see him, and *you* didn't allow it?" She shook her head. "I don't think you can gatekeep this. We will always be here for him. But is it fair to keep that knowledge from him? Doesn't Chirag deserve to change and grow and come back?"

Karina had said as much to Aneel about Saira and his dad. Oh god. The look on Aneel's face when he realized that Chirag was still in love with her. The pain and hurt—he couldn't even speak. And she'd had nothing to offer him.

Karina felt like crap the next morning. Her head pounded. Her stomach roiled with nausea. What had she been thinking, drinking almost two bottles of wine by herself?

And then she remembered the events of the evening.

Well, maybe that was why.

She dragged herself out of bed. Got Veer off to school. And then just sat. No one was home. She went over the events of last night in her mind.

She knew in her heart that she would have to let Chirag and Veer meet.

Her phone buzzed. It was a text from Aneel.

Hey, I'm at the farmers market. Tell me what you need. I'm sure the wine did not treat you well last night.

Oh crap. Karina sat straight up on the sofa. She had completely forgotten that she had won the challenge yesterday, and she was running the kitchen for the week. She texted him back.

On my way. Be there in 20.

She threw on some clothes, grabbed a paratha and downed some Advil before racing out the door.

Her phone buzzed again.

I got the tomatoes you like and the onions. The cilantro looks awful. I'll stop at the Indian store for that.

She sent a thumbs-up. He knew which tomatoes she liked. She smiled at her phone as her heart warmed at that fact. She pushed aside all the other warm feelings he brought about.

She couldn't deal with all that now. She'd seen Chirag once, and already her rhythm was off.

She parked at the market, noting that the camera crew wasn't there. They usually liked to have footage of the shopping.

She donned her sunglasses and put her hair up in a ponytail, heading for the produce section. If he had onion and tomatoes, he'd be looking at leafy greens right now. Sure enough, she caught his head of dark hair, sporting his beloved aviators and a fitted Iron Man shirt, leaning over the kale. As she got closer, she saw that it wasn't an Iron Man shirt. It was Captain America.

"Hey," she said as she approached. He made quite the attractive picture, tight T-shirt, sunglasses, mussed hair, buying vegetables. She couldn't read his eyes, but his mouth, pressed together in a tight smile of greeting, spoke volumes.

"Sorry about being late," she added.

Aneel just nodded, barely looking her way. "How much kale do you need?" were his first words to her.

She told him, and the vendor packed it up for them. They moved to the next stall, and she felt his gaze over her face. "How bad is that headache?" A small smirk made a showing.

"I'll deal," she said. "Where's the camera crew?"

"I convinced them that they did not need to be here for this. I figured you would have a world-class headache and might not want cameras in your face, so we get to shop in private today. Warning, though, they will be waiting for you for hair and makeup when we get to the restaurant."

She gaped at him. She couldn't remember the last time anyone had put her needs forward like this. She started walking. "Thank you."

Aneel handed her a bottle of a light pink liquid. "Pink grapefruit electrolytes."

She drank from it, the tart drink surprisingly soothing. "Though a real friend would have taken the wine away from me." She smirked at him.

He shook his head, glancing her way. "Not worth my life to take wine away from you." They took a few steps in silence. "So we're back to being just friends?" He clearly tried to mask the pain in his voice. He did not succeed.

"I am letting Chirag and Veer meet. My feelings aside, they need to have their own relationship." She focused on him. "To be honest, it was what you said about hating your father for the past twenty years that made me decide."

"What about it?"

"I don't want Veer to hate his father. At least this way, they can get to know each other and decide for themselves."

Aneel nodded, a slight frown on those luscious lips. She tried not to think about how those lips had felt against her neck. She failed.

"You think my hatred of my father harms me more than him?" Aneel asked, looking at her through his sunglasses.

Karina sighed. "I do, Sunshine. Hatred really harms the person who carries it the most. If you want to let it go, you need to meet with him."

He frowned but nodded. "You didn't answer my question," he said, his voice quiet. "Are we back to being just friends?"

Karina swallowed hard. She did not want to be friends with him. She had a taste of what it was like to love him and be loved by him, and she *needed* that. "Chirag is looking to be a family. What kind of mother would I be if I didn't even consider it?"

"Do you love him?" The words were ground out.

"I did at one time."

"That's not an answer."

"It's all I have." She drank from the bottle he had given her.

She couldn't see his eyes, but his gaze was over her head. "Feeling better?" he asked. His voice was distant, clinical, devoid of warmth.

She nodded.

"Let's finish up here and head back. We have a restaurant to run."

Though he did not move, Karina felt the distance between them. She shivered despite the unusually warm morning.

Karina knew exactly what she wanted from the market, unlike Aneel, who always decided what he wanted when he got to the farmers market. She was a faster shopper. Which helped today, so they were able to make up the time she had lost.

At the restaurant, they cooked together, as they had the past four weeks, regardless of who was appointed head chef that week. They had already learned each other's habits, strengths and weaknesses, easily falling into a rhythm in the kitchen.

To his credit, Aneel asked no further questions about Veer or Chirag, which helped keep her focused on the job at hand.

Though neither one of them had said it, they knew they were two-for-two for the weekly challenges, and that the judges, along with Deepak, were watching them closely to determine who got the head chef position.

Karina gave it her full effort, though something tugged at her. Maybe... Aneel was right. Even as she prepared her menu for the restaurant, her thoughts kept jumping to the parties she had going on this weekend. Any thoughts of Chirag she pushed aside for the time being.

Even today, she'd gotten at least three emails requesting her services. Two emails were people who had watched the show, were impressed with her ideas. The third was from her gig with Mrs. Arora. How funny would it be that the position she had been interested in actually led her to catering?

If she applied herself, made a business plan, she could really make it work. She pushed aside those thoughts for now. It was nearly 4:00 p.m., and they needed to start the evening.

She cleared her mind of everything but the cooking.

Aneel watched Karina. He watched as her focus narrowed to only the restaurant. He envied her that. All he could think about was that when he asked if she loved Chirag, she didn't say no. That and the fact that he should see his own father.

The evening wore on and on. It was endless. Karina might have been focused on the restaurant, but his focus was squarely on her.

They finished out the evening to nothing but praise. "Chef Mistry," Deepak said. "Well done."

"I could not have done it without Chef Rawal, to be honest. He's very talented and inspirational," Karina told them, her smile genuine.

Deepak glanced between the two of them, obviously confused. But he said no more and left.

Aneel and Karina helped the staff clean up as they always did, the banter and the gossip always relaxing after a long evening.

Rakesh popped his head into the kitchen as they were finishing up. "You two are neck and neck. The viewers love you both. It's literally a tie. Business is up. After talking to Deepak, we're going to extend the competition one week. One more cook-off, and that'll be the tiebreaker."

Both Aneel and Karina raised their voices to protest. Rakesh held up his hands. "We are having a tie-breaker." He walked out.

They finished up, and Aneel waited for Karina in the locker room as he always did.

"I thought you'd be gone by now," Karina said softly.

He simply stood and waited while she gathered her things. Aneel walked her to her car as he did every night, tonight in silence. The memory of kissing her in front of this car just yesterday was both fresh and distant.

They stopped as she unlocked the door, a small beep the only sound. She turned to him. "I'm sorry. This...whole thing...isn't fair to you. I know I said I wanted to give us a chance... I just... You don't have to do all this. And you certainly do not have to help me cater for the weekend."

"There will never be a time that I don't walk you to your car." He met her gaze, focusing on those hazel eyes that hid nothing. "There will never be a time when I do not come when you call." He stepped closer to her. "I learned a long time ago that life isn't fair. This has nothing to do with being fair. I love you, and that's just how it is."

Her lips parted and her eyes softened at his confession.

He couldn't stop himself. He didn't want to stop himself. "The fact of my love for you is just that—fact. Just as surely as you are Grumpy." He offered her a half smile. "And I am Sunshine, it *is*. I started falling for you when we first met seven years ago. Seeing you here, now..." he met her gaze with his, so there was no doubt that what he said was true "...was just an opportunity to fall for you again."

She just stared at him. "I... I..." Her eyes glistened under the light of the street lamp.

He leaned down and brushed his lips over her cheek. "Get in your car. Go home. I'll see you in the morning to work on the catering."

He watched her drive away as he got in his own car. She was going to break his heart into a thousand pieces, which he would never be able to put together again.

And he was going to let her.

Aneel arrived home to find Saira sitting in front of her computer, the new puppy at her feet.

"How'd it go today?" she asked without turning. The puppy raised her head and ran to Aneel, sniffing him.

He picked up the tiny animal. "Did you name this little heart breaker?"

Saira sighed and shook her head. "No. Turns out the shelter found her a home. A little girl had seen her before me, and then she came back and was heartbroken that this dog was gone..." Saira shook her head. "It's a whole thing." She sighed. "Anyway, I'd feel terrible knowing this little girl wanted her. To be fair, the shelter had warned me this might happen. But people almost never come back. I'll drop her off tomorrow." The disappointment in Saira's voice was real.

Aneel walked over and kissed the top of her head. "There will be another puppy meant for you."

Saira looked up at him amd smiled while she shook her head. "You didn't answer my question."

Aneel sat on the sofa with the dog in his lap without even taking off his shoes.

"Shoes, Bhaiya," his sister scolded.

He removed his shoes and stayed on the sofa. The light weight of the tiny fur ball in his lap comforting him. He heard Saira clicking away for a moment. Then she came and sat next to him.

"Something has happened."

"I did what you said—and you were right. She gave me a chance." He grinned at his sister. "Then her ex—Veer's father—showed up. He wants to see Veer, and he claims he still loves Karina."

"Does she still love him?"

"I don't know." He sighed. "She's going to let her son meet his father, so that he doesn't end up possibly hating his dad for twenty years." He side-eyed his sister.

"You're right, she's a smart woman," Saira said.

"She said something about hate eating the person who holds it." He kept petting the dog.

"Also true." Saira smirked at him. "You need to marry this woman."

"There's nothing I want to do more." He hadn't been thinking in terms of marriage, but he had seen a future with Karina and Veer. But now that Saira mentioned it, he wanted that future with a longing that was painful. "She has to figure out her stuff."

"While she's doing that, Bhaiya, why don't you figure out yours?"

The puppy jumped onto the floor, and Aneel turned to his sister. "What do you know?"

"Everything."

The puppy sniffed around in a circle.

"Tell me."

"No." She looked him in the eye.

"No?"

"If you want to know, call him. Have coffee and give him a chance to explain." She stood, reaching for the puppy too late. A puddle of pee was already growing on the floor. She sighed. "Did you at least learn that French toast recipe before you set her free?"

Chapter Thirty-Two

The next few days were a blur of cooking for the party on the weekend as well as running the restaurant. In both areas, Aneel was nothing less than her full partner. He stayed up late with her, cooked with her, planned with her. While he did not distance himself from Veer, he seemed to be making sure that he only came around when Veer was sleeping or at school.

Veer kept asking her when they would watch another Avengers movie with Aneel. She had no answer. Instead, she talked to him about his dad,

"So, Veer. Your dad has been away for a while, but now he's back. And he would like to meet you. What do you think?"

Veer stared at his mother in silence for a minute. "Do you think he likes Avengers?"

"I don't know," Karina answered honestly. "Does that matter to you?"

"Hmm. Not really. But it would be fun if he did," Veer said.

"So do you want to meet him?"

Veer nodded enthusiastically. "Yes. But…"

"But what?"

"Can Aneel Uncle come? I haven't seen him in a while," Veer said.

"Maybe another time." Karina smiled at her son, even as a pang in her heart caused her pain. "Let me text your father and see when he's free."

* * *

Karina was enjoying a quiet, restorative Sunday afternoon when the front doorbell rang. Veer was at a playdate, Sona was at a shoot, her father was with his girlfriend. She answered to find Saira. Though she'd be lying if she hadn't hoped for Aneel.

"Hi. I hope this isn't a bad time." Saira looked nervous.

"No. All good. No one's home." Karina stepped aside to let her in.

"So I'm interrupting your alone time. I'll come back." Saira started to leave.

"Don't be ridiculous. I'm happy to see you." And Karina was. Any connection to Aneel. She was pathetic. "Though you might be here to yell at me."

Saira shook her head as she came in. "No. Aneel is a grown man—well, most of the time anyway. What happened with you two is up to, well, you two."

Karina led the way into the kitchen and pulled out a bottle of wine and held it up in question.

"Yes, please," Saira answered.

Karina poured the glasses and took them to the sofa. Saira followed. They clinked glasses and sipped.

"So. What can I do for you?" Karina asked.

Saira took a large gulp of her wine and looked at Karina, her eyes wide.

Something in Karina jolted. Saira had something to tell her. Something big.

"Well, I know that I said what happens between you two is up to you, but I need you to have all the facts," the young girl started.

Karina sipped her wine and looked at her, trying not to look panicked. "Okay. Should I be afraid?"

"No. I should be."

Karina furrowed her brow.

Saira took another large gulp of her wine. "Here's the thing. My brother never cheated. At that competition. He really didn't need to—and besides, that's just not him."

"I know." Karina nodded her head. "I know that's just not him."

"What you don't know is that it was me."

Karina froze. Of all the things she could have thought Saira was going to say, this was not one of them.

Saira continued, "I didn't know he was going to use the money for me. My brother had a dream of going to culinary school. That was all I wanted for him. He entered that competition. I knew he was going to win. He needed to win. He was good. But you, you were also so, so good. The competition was so close. I wanted to make sure that after all these years of taking care of me and taking care of my mom and doing all those things that he finally got something for him." Saira paused but maintained eye contact with Karina. "So I sneaked in. After everybody was gone. And *I* pulled that plug. I also had made sure that he didn't make anything that needed to be refrigerated."

Karina just stared at her.

Saira looked at her. "Please say something, and please don't hold this against my brother."

"One question."

"Yes?"

"Did your brother know?"

Saira shook her head. "I've never been able to tell him." She pressed her lips together. "I'm telling you first."

Karina was silent. There *had* been cheating. This validation of her suspicion did not satisfy her the way she thought it would. She had always thought she would feel some level of victory in finding out the truth. But she did not.

Turning to Saira, she said firmly, "Truthfully, I could have used that 30K as well."

Saira had the grace to look ashamed.

"What you did was wrong." Karina paused as she continued to process this information. No surge of anger, just some irritation. "But I have sisters who I would die for, so I can appreciate that you did this out of love for your brother." She inhaled and softened. "Coming here to tell me this, even now, when you didn't have to, is honest, and I respect that." Karina smiled at the youg woman.

"Please don't hold this against him," Saira said, her normally strong voice not much more than a squeak.

"I have let it go. Only recently, but still," Karina confessed.

"It's just...you make him happier than I've almost ever seen him," Saira said softly. "Just so you know."

Karina could not help the smile on her face any more than she could help the lightness in her heart.

"He makes you happy, too." Saira smiled as this revelation hit her.

Karina pressed her lips together. How Aneel Rawal made her feel was nobody's business. Least of all the sister who loved him. Her feelings for Aneel were irrelevant when compared to Veer's needs. "I know you want your brother to be happy. I appreciate your honesty today. But I may not be the person for Aneel. There's a lot..." Karina shook her head. "There's just a lot."

Saira nodded and stood. "Sure. I get it. Like I said, it's between you two. But I think you should know that you have had an impact on him."

"Why do you say that?"

"Because right now he's out. Meeting with our dad."

"Thanks for meeting with me." Yogesh Rawal looked older than his years, but Aneel supposed that excessive alcohol use would do that to a man. Though much like the last time he'd seen Yogesh Rawal, there did not seem to be evidence of the man having had anything to drink recently. He was clean, clear eyed and well dressed.

They found a small table in the corner and sat down with their coffees.

"Well, my sister insisted that I at least hear you out." Aneel leveled the man with the hardest stare he could muster. *The woman he was in love with thought so, too.* "And I'll do anything for my sister."

His father nodded. "Your sister speaks highly of you. Your mom raised you well."

Aneel nodded, opened his hands. "What's the story?"

"Your mom kicked me out when you were ten. Not without reason. But it wasn't just because I drank too much. That was the symptom. The problem was depression. But instead of getting the help I needed, I self-medicated with alcohol. Your mother, she knew this, she begged me to get help. She even made appointments for me, but I always found an excuse not to go. Don't ask why, I hardly know myself. Pride was most of it. The alcohol helped, or so I thought.

"She didn't toss me onto the streets. There was an accident…" Yogesh looked away from him, as if he couldn't meet Aneel's eyes. "The accident spurred me to finally take responsibility, to take care of myself. I entered a program that helped me get sober, then get counseling for the depression." He looked at Aneel.

Aneel remained stoic.

"Sometime later, I returned to your mother, but she was done with me. We divorced, and I did not fight her when she wanted full custody. She made it clear that I was not welcome anymore. Given the trauma I had put you all through, I was loathe to force it at the time. When she died and you refused me, I was heartbroken, but again, I did not wish to further hurt you and Saira."

"Why come now?" Aneel asked, his eyes narrowed.

"Saira found me and reached out," he said. "She wanted to meet me, she said. I was thrilled, so I agreed."

"What do you do now?" Aneel ran his gaze over the man. Clearly he was now sober and gainfully employed.

"I had studied to be a computer engineer. I now work at a tech company," his father answered. "I wanted you and your sister to know that we have this history of depression in our family. When I look back, it's clear to me now that what I thought was just a family of heavy drinkers was people trying to deal with their depression."

Aneel nodded. He didn't know how to feel right now.

"My biggest regret, and I have many, is losing the time with you and Saira." Tears lined his father's eyes. Aneel fought to remain unmoved. "I look at you both now, and I see what an amazing job your mother did with you. I have never known anyone as strong as her, and I see her strength and love in the both you."

The ice around Aneel's heart melted a bit at the mention of his mother and his father's obvious regrets and vulnerability.

His mother had only been trying to protect him and Saira. Much like Karina had considered. He tried not to think about how life might be different if his mother had at least let them see that their father hadn't simply randomly abandoned them. How would he be different if he hadn't spent twenty years angry at the man in front of him? If he had known the truth. He didn't blame his mother—not for a minute. She had done what was best for them with information she had. She had protected them. His mind bounced to Karina. She was doing what she thought was best for Veer. Saving him from twenty years of anger. In spite of every bit of anger Aneel had harbored all these years, he softened a bit toward the man in front of him. No one was more surprised than him that he was even capable of that softness. He studied the man across from him as he drank his coffee.

There was more. Aneel could feel it.

His father set down his coffee cup and looked at Aneel. "I also want to tell you that I'm getting remarried."

The new soft feelings hardened once more, as something ugly built inside him. Though he wasn't sure why he should care, why he should feel anger or betrayal or abandonment from a man he had no relationship with. Whatever it was, it was overpowering, and he found it hard to sit here.

Aneel stood, all the softness gone from him. "Have a nice life." He turned on his heel and left.

Chapter Thirty-Three

Monday rolled around, and Karina showed up ready for the tiebreaker. She brought Veer with her as there was no school again today, and the family was busy. Aneel was a bit late, his brow furrowed as he entered the locker room. But he beamed upon seeing Veer in the locker room.

"Hey, no school today?" Aneel addressed Veer, glancing at Karina.

Veer was coloring and looked up, his eyes widening. "Aneel Uncle." He squealed and jumped up to hug him. "No school and then later Mom's taking me—"

"Hey." Deepak peeked in the locker room. "We need to get started."

They both quickly and silently put on their whites, presented themselves in front of the judges in their respective spots as they had for the past four weeks and waited to hear what their assignment was.

Sonny Pandya stood. "I know that you have been called here for a tiebreaker. But the judges and I have been talking, and we've seen what the viewers have said. And to be honest, it really doesn't matter what would happen in this tiebreaker competition. We have observed the two of you working this restaurant for the past month. It is abundantly clear that the two of you work beautifully in tandem with one another. There is no ego. There is only a partnership, and that is what has made this restaurant run so well for the past four weeks. All of that to say that we do not pick a head chef. We pick this partnership. We choose the both of you to run this restaurant just as you have been doing for the past month."

Karina stood there speechless. Aneel also said nothing. They looked at each other. Karina knew that he knew what she was thinking. He nodded at her. She stepped forward.

"Thank you so much for that. We have truly enjoyed working together this month. But we've both learned things. I, for one, learned that I'm a happier as a caterer than I am running the restaurant."

Aneel stepped up. "And I have learned that I love running this kitchen."

Aneel and Karina looked at each other.

Karina spoke first. "Thank you so much for the opportunity, but I respectfully decline."

Aneel grinned at her, then looked at the judges. "Thank you for the opportunity. And if you still want me, even without Chef Mistry, I will respectfully accept."

All three judges and Deepak looked at each other.

Divya Shah spoke first. "I've seen her catering. She's incredible. Come find me after, Chef Mistry, we'll talk."

Aneel looked at Deepak. "What do you say?"

Deepak shook his head. "I said from the beginning I was more than happy with either of you. I just did not want to make that decision. Chef Rawal, welcome to Fusion. You are now the new executive chef."

Aneel caught Karina's eye and turned to the judges. "We're here. Want us to make you one last quick lunch?"

"That would be divine," Divya said.

Karina turned to Aneel. "Dabeli? Those ones you made tasted straight from the cart."

"You read my mind, Chef."

They got to work. Divya came over to Karina as she

chopped onions. "Hey. Thank you for the vote of confidence," Karina said.

"Of course. Listen, Amar and I get swamped with catering gigs. Are you planning on going out on your own or working for someone?"

"Well, I planned on continuing from home so I have the flexibility of being with my son. He's four."

"Amar and I work from our home as well, but we get swamped with large weddings for five hundred plus, and it's a lot. Would you be interested in helping out or working with us when needed? We can be flexible with the schedule. It would also be great to be able to network with one another, you know?"

Karina beamed. "I would love that. Thank you."

"Get settled and reach out to me next week to discuss details. Amar and I are taking the weekend off." Divya giggled. "And by the way, your kulfi—amazing." She went back to the judges table and started talking to Amar.

"Hey, Chef." Aneel leaned over. "Not bad. Building a relationship with Amar Virani and Divya Shah."

Karina beamed. "Congrats to you, too, Head Chef Rawal. Thanks again for helping me out." She paused. "Your sister came to see me yesterday."

"Did she?" He snapped his focus to her. "What did she want?"

"Girl talk." Karina raised her eyebrows at him.

"Hmm." Aneel was suddenly interested in his potatoes.

"She mentioned that you saw your dad." Karina flicked her gaze to him.

Aneel nodded, but his body went stiff.

"How did it go?" she asked.

Aneel sighed, a deep and heavy thing.

"Tell me the whole story."

He filled her in as they cooked.

"Well, he has depression that he seems to be handling, and he's not wrong, you need to know that it runs in your family. You and Saira," Karina said thoughtfully.

"I get that," he said slowly, something simmering beneath the surface there.

"There's more?" Karina stopped working for a moment and looked at him.

"He's getting married."

Karina's eyes popped open.

"My mom suffered all those years he refused to get help. Now that he's a better man, he gets a happily-ever-after with someone else? Where was my mother's happy ending?" Aneel was fuming at the injustice to his mother. He shook his head. "It's too much."

Karina went back to work, her heart aching as she watched him struggle. He clearly wanted to forgive his father, but he was so angry that his mother never had her moment in the sun.

They finished cooking and served up their dabeli sandwiches to the judges and staff to compliments all around.

"Chef Rawal," Sonny Pandya called out.

Aneel turned away from the cleanup and held out his hand. "Aneel."

Sonny shook it. "I believe we can share recipes now."

Aneel offered his signature smile. "That we can. I'd love to do something in conjunction with the Masala Hut."

Sonny grinned. "Let's set it up."

"Thanks, by the way," Karina said. "For sending Sangeeta my way for that wedding."

"Of course. Glad it worked out. Sangeeta was quite stressed about it." He smiled. "I know it means a lot to her that you agreed to help out."

Aneel and Karina made their way back to the locker room to find Veer still coloring, one of the line cooks keeping him company. "What's going on today?" Aneel asked him.

"Mom's taking me to meet my dad," Veer said.

Aneel snapped his head to Karina.

"We're…" She cleared her throat and averted her eyes. "Meeting him for a late lunch," she explained.

"That's great," Aneel told Veer. "Really exciting."

Veer shrugged.

Aneel looked at Karina, she nodded. Aneel knelt in front of Veer. "You're not excited," he said softly.

"I am." Veer furrowed his brow. "It's just…" He threw a furtive glance at his mother. Karina held up her hands and stepped back to give him privacy, though she could still hear him.

"It's just what?" Aneel asked gently, as if he had all the time in the world.

"What if I don't know what to say? What if… what if he doesn't like me?" Veer's normally enthusiastic voice was quiet and subdued.

Karina fought the urge to grab her son into her arms and just cancel with Chirag.

"Well," said Aneel. "Two things. One." He took Veer's hand and held one of his fingers. "Just say whatever you feel like. You are great at talking to people. Don't you remember the first time we met, we talked the whole time? And I like you just fine."

Veer nodded and a small smile crept to his face.

"Two." Veer held up a second finger, and Aneel smiled his approval. "Of course he's going to like you. Fathers always like their sons, no matter what." He caught Karina's eye. "And sons, well, they just have to give their dads a chance."

"What does that mean?" Veer asked.

"That means you just say hi and then do what feels right." Aneel placed his hand over Veer's heart.

"Can you come with us?"

Aneel chuckled. "No, buddy. You have your mom. You're going to be fine."

Veer looked at Aneel as if he were trying to see if Aneel was bullshitting him. Then he nodded. He reached his arms around Aneel's neck. "Thank you."

Aneel hugged him back and stood with Veer still wrapped around his neck. "I have something stuck around my neck," Aneel said.

This resulted in giggles from Veer, just as Aneel had clearly anticipated.

Karina met his eyes, put a hand over her heart and mouthed a thank-you to him.

He grinned back at her, but she didn't miss the touch of sadness in his eyes.

Karina and Veer went home for a quick clothing change. By the time they got home, Veer was excited, choosing clothes, asking questions. She was giving Chirag exactly one chance. If he hurt Veer, they were done.

Karina parked the car in front of the restaurant.

"Mom! Check it out!" Veer's eyes bugged out at a limo parked a few spaces down from them.

Karina's stomach was in knots as she spared the limo a glance and managed a smile for Veer. How would Chirag react? How would Veer react? Aneel's voice came to her. *Breathe.* She inhaled and exhaled deeply. Neither of their reactions were under her control. She would just have to deal with whatever unfolded here today.

By the time she opened the door, she was feeling a bit more centered.

The restaurant was beautiful. Quiet atmosphere, the light clinking of glass and silverware and the soft murmur of conversation were the only sounds. Linens and silverware and proper manners required.

Veer was unfazed. He just wanted to meet his dad. Karina and Veer walked up to find Chirag already seated, but he stood as they approached. He was dashing in a dark navy suit and crisp white shirt. He had forgone the tie, but the reality was that the man was wearing a suit to meet his four-year-old son.

Veer looked up at him.

Chirag knelt to his eye level and extended his hand. "Hi, Veer."

Veer eyed him and shook his hand. "Hi." Her very excited child was suddenly apprehensive, glancing around the restaurant, taking it all in.

Chirag followed his gaze and frowned. "You know what? I'm not sure I feel like eating here. Where do you like to eat, Veer?"

Veer looked at his mother, the question in his eyes.

"It's okay. Go ahead and tell him." She smiled, encouraging him.

"I love McDonald's," Veer said.

Chirag chuckled. "Quarter pounder with cheese sounds great right about now. McDonald's it is." He stood, and they left the restaurant.

"I like regular hamburgers," Veer said. "Mom likes the cheeseburger."

They walked out, and Chirag opened the door to the limo. Veer widened his eyes at his mother, beside himself with excitement. His first limo ride ever.

Veer pushed all the buttons, waving to the driver when the partition lowered. He fingered the glassware, being careful not to pick any of it up.

They got McDonald's to go and ate in the limo as they toured Baltimore. Karina forced herself to sit still, to not rein in his curiosity and was pleasantly surprised that Chirag did not seem to be bothered by Veer's enthusiasm in the least. Chirag didn't even bat an eyelash when a few fries fell to the floor, or when greasy fingers touched the upholstery.

They ended up going to the aquarium, where Chirag indulged Veer's current obsession with turtles and the 'finding nemo' fish.

Chirag was relaxed and amusing. Similar to the guy she'd known all those years ago but more responsible, more focused. Veer was talking nonstop, any fear of not knowing what to say evaporated away. Chirag appeared to be completely tickled. She caught Chirag watching her, and she gave him an encouraging nod.

All in all, the afternoon was pretty wonderful.

"So, did you get chosen for executive chef?" Chirag asked her as they walked around a park while Veer played on the jungle gym.

"Yes, I did." She explained what had happened. "But I turned it down. I prefer to move forward with my catering business. I enjoy it more, and it gives me flexibility for Veer."

"The executive chef position seems more lucrative, more stable," Chirag said. "But I'm here for Veer now, too."

She froze, her stomach clenched. "What do you mean?"

He looked at her and gasped. "No. Karina. I'm not here to take Veer from you. Regardless of what happens between us—I would not dream of hurting either of you that way. I'm just looking to be part of his life."

"Really?" Karina asked. She hadn't realized how true that fear was until this moment. The fear that Chirag would use his apparent wealth to take Veer from her.

Chirag nodded. "Really." He paused. "And if possible, part of yours as well."

Karina relaxed.

Chirag leaned toward her, and the scent of his cologne took her back in time to when they'd been together. "Thank you so much for this. He's wonderful. You and your family have done a fabulous job with him."

"He kind of came out that wonderful."

"You made him more so."

They watched Veer play for a bit in silence.

Chirag looked at her. "Would you consider having dinner with me?"

She stared at him a moment. She'd had feelings for him once. Maybe they were still there. She glanced at Veer. Maybe she owed it to Veer to find out. "Yes. Dinner would be great."

Chapter Thirty-Four

Aneel knocked on the mudroom door that had in such a short time become as familiar to him as his own apartment door. There was a faint "come in" from Karina in the kitchen. Fusion was closed for a week to deep clean and organize after the TV show, so Aneel had some extra time on his hands.

He entered, removing his shoes. The aroma of roasting spices hit, and he was immediately calmer. "Hey. You got started without me," he said.

"Literally been five minutes." Karina smiled, calming him further. "I didn't take the good part away from you."

He grinned. He loved to add a little something unexpected to certain mixtures. "You know me so well."

"Well, the last time I roasted and ground spices without you, Sunshine, you basically pouted." She put her hands on her hips and raised an eyebrow.

"Exaggerations. I don't pout."

"Guess again," she said.

They worked in silence for a few minutes.

"How did it go with Veer and his dad?" It had to be asked. Though the real question was, *How did it go with you and your ex who still loves you?*

Karina's face lit up. "Fabulous. Veer had a great time. Though what kid wouldn't? Chirag got us McDonald's in his limo." She laughed. "Veer talked nonstop, and Chirag was totally there for it."

"That's fabulous," he said, forcing encouragement into his voice. He was happy that the meeting had gone well for Veer and that Chirag seemed to be really stepping up—at least so far in doing what Veer would like. The pit in his belly was from wondering if Karina's laugh was a mother's happiness or a woman's.

"At first, I was concerned that Chirag was trying to buy his love, but that wasn't the vibe at all. He is definitely well-off, but when it comes to Veer, he's not just about the money."

"Sounds like a win-win," Aneel said as he gathered more spices to roast. *Don't ask if she hit it off with Chirag. Be strong! Don't ask.* He swallowed the question.

"It really was." She leaned on the counter and looked at him. "Your little talk with him really helped."

"Yeah?"

"Of course, it did. Veer really likes you," Karina said.

Aneel's heart warmed at that, and he met her eyes. "That makes me feel—I don't know." He put a hand to his chest. "Great."

She held his gaze, and he knew the question was in his eyes, but he didn't ask it. She had to figure out her life without him clawing at her. He looked away.

"So, where are we on this big wedding prep?" he asked so they had something else to focus on besides the fact that he was pining for her.

She cleared her throat and looked away, busying herself with invisible dust on the counter. "I went to the farmers market for the wedding yesterday, so once we get these spices ready, we're good until Saturday. I have staff coming early Saturday to the venue to work on chopping. Want to come with me to the final meeting with the bride since Fusion is closed? Tomorrow?"

He would never say no to doing anything with her. "Yes. Get a final feel for it all. Let's go over everything."

She pulled out her laptop, and they went over each item in detail.

"You're doing the Thai-influenced samosa thing." He added some cockiness to his voice. "Finally realized the wonder that is fusion cuisine."

She rolled her eyes. "I draw the line at Tater Tots at a wedding."

Before they knew it, the mudroom door banged open, and Veer came barreling in. "Aneel Uncle, Aneel Uncle, I saw your car outside." He ran in and threw his arms around Aneel's legs, just as Aneel had seen him do so many times to Param and his grandfather.

"Hey! How was school?" Aneel got down on his knees.

"School was great. But I want you to meet my dad." Veer beamed up at Aneel as he pointed to Chirag. "This my dad. And this is Aneel Uncle."

"Hey," Chirag said. Extending his hand. "We met at the party. You work with Karina." He grinned.

"Right," Aneel said, standing and forcing a smile before he shook Chirag's hand. "We work together." Colleagues. They were only colleagues. Who made out a few times.

"Aneel Uncle. We were in a limo yesterday," Veer told him.

"No way!" Aneel's laugh with Veer was real.

"Yes! And then…" Veer caught him up on all his activities since they had last seen each other, then dumped his backpack to show him what they'd done in school.

Aneel sat on the floor and enjoyed every minute, though he was aware of the soft voices behind him as Karina and Chirag chatted. Was that Karina *giggling?* His heart dropped. Aneel put his focus on Veer until the boy had finished.

Aneel stood as Karina took Veer's hand and led him to the

family room and upstairs. Aneel forced a grin in Chirag's direction. "Looks like Veer had a great time."

"I hope so," Chirag said, leaning against the counter. "So, congratulations to you. I hear you're the new executive chef."

Aneel nodded. "Thank you. It's certainly an exciting time."

Karina returned. "Can I get you anything, Chirag? Coffee, chai?"

Chirag focused his attention on her. "Chai would be great," he said softly.

This was Aneel's cue to leave. "I better get going."

"Oh, I was going to make coffee as well, if you want to stay. We need to finish looking at the menu." Karina met Aneel's eyes, Chirag's gaze was fixed firmly on her.

"No. I should get back." No way was he going to be able to drink coffee while Chirag made googly eyes at Karina. He could almost hear his heart breaking. "Just email me the menu, I'll take a pass at it tonight, but I'm sure it's wonderful." He extended a hand to Chirag, then glanced at Karina. "Tomorrow. The meeting. Just text me the address."

Aneel crawled out of bed the next morning and stood under the shower for an extended period of time in an attempt to feel half alive for this meeting. He would, of course, help Karina with this wedding, despite the fact that Tyler was of the opinion that Aneel should basically just rip-off the Band-Aid and part ways with Karina, for his own best interest.

Unbidden, memories from growing up floated through his mind. Playing with Saira. Fighting with Saira. Helping her with homework. Learning how to chop from his mother. His irritation when he learned she never measured anything while cooking. His mom's hand gently brushing back the hair from his forehead. The sense of pride he felt the first time he successfully made dhal to feed his mom.

He turned off the water, feeling more awake. He dressed and readied himself to meet Karina.

Chirag was rich, kind, supposedly handsome. Most important, he was Veer's father. Aneel just needed to move forward. Move on with his life as it was. He was the executive chef at a restaurant, Saira was all but finished her education. It was time to focus on himself.

He paused a moment as a realization fell upon him. All this time, he had been angry that his mother never really got her 'happily-ever-after'. Except that she did. He and Saira loved each other fiercely. And now, Saira was on the verge of fulfilling her dream of being a veterinarian, and he just landed his dream job. Thanks, in large part to his mom, and all that time they spent together in the kitchen.

His heart still ached for Karina, his still missed his mother. All that angst he carried about his mother never having happiness dimmed as he saw his mother's life in new light. Karina made almost all her decisions based on Veer's happiness. If Veer was happy, Karina was happy. It was possible that his mother had felt the same way. As long as he and Saira were happy, so was she. It wasn't everything, but it was some form of happiness for her.

Saira was not convinced that Karina had chosen Chirag, but she didn't know Karina like he did. Didn't know how a parent would think.

It would do him no good to focus on Karina and Chirag at the moment. He would go to this meeting and help cater the wedding this weekend. He had declared that he would always be there for Karina. He simply hadn't realized how painful that would be.

Aneel dressed and came out to find his sister sitting at their formica table having chai and tepla.

"Hey. Don't you have clinic?" She startled when he spoke.

"You okay?" He asked coming closer. Her eyes were wide and she was watching him with clear apprehension.

Something had happened.

She slid a mug toward him and motioned for him to sit. "I have the later shift."

He sat down and sipped the chai, his eyes never leaving hers, and waited.

"Bhaiya." Her voice cracked and she stopped.

His heart thudded in his chest. "Spit it out Saira."

She swallowed and nodded. "I went to see Karina the other day." Aneel waited.

"I had to tell her the truth about that competition." Tears swam in his sister's eyes.

What the—

"It was me," Saira blurted out. "I was the one who unplugged the refrigerator."

Aneel blinked. Of all the things that Saira could have said, this was not remotely what he might have guessed.

"I just wanted you to have something. You took care of me, and mom. I wanted you to have that money so you could do something for yourself." She paused. "I'm so sorry. I know it was wrong and I wanted to tell you so many times, but I was afraid."

Any number of lectures came to mind. *It was wrong. It was cheating. You should not have done that.*

"Afraid of what?"

"That you would hate me."

"I could never hate you." His sister was filled with remorse, that much was clear. "What did Karina say?"

"She wasn't happy. But she said she understood that I did it because I loved you. She was actually pretty great about it."

Aneel nodded. Of course she was. Karina understood that sibling bond.

"Say something, Bhaiya."

"I wish you hadn't felt the need to do that—"

"You worked so hard," his sister said.

He nodded and finished his chai. "I need to go."

"I am truly sorry." Her lower lip trembled, but she didn't cry.

"I know you are," he said gently. "If Karina has put it in the past, then we can, too."

She snapped her gaze at him, hope in her eyes. "Really?"

He nodded and smiled. "Really."

Saira stood and gave him a huge hug, like the ones he gave when she was little. "You're the best."

"So I have been told," he said with a small chuckle.

"I need to go." Her confession over, Saira's energy seemed to be back in full force.

"Work hard," he said.

"Of course," Saira said as she left.

Aneel checked in with his restaurant—that felt good, at least. All was well, so he pushed aside this newest revelation and donned his good chef's whites and drove to the venue.

They were meeting at a large, gorgeous hotel on the water on the eastern shore of Maryland. Clearly, the couple had spared no expense. When Aneel arrived, Karina was already there in her chef's whites, talking to a woman he assumed was the planner.

"Hey," Karina greeted him as he approached. She did a double take and then rested her gaze on him.

He tamped down the excitement he felt from her attention to him. Karina, for her part, looked positively radiant.

"Hey. Sorry, I hope I'm not late," Aneel said, not acknowledging her tone. He stopped and whispered, "Saira just confessed…"

Karina gave him a small smile. "It happened. It's over. Let's leave it in the past."

Aneel upturned his lips. "I knew I—" *Loved you for a reason.* "Well, I'm happy you understand."

Karina's eyes softened as if she knew what he had really wanted to say. She tugged at his sleeve. "The planner is waiting for us." She led the way.

"This is the planner, Sangeeta Parikh," Karina started. "Sangeeta, this is Aneel, my—"

"Assistant?" he cut in.

Karina smiled. "Let's go with that." She leaned toward him. "I was going to say friend."

He simply glanced at her. That would have hurt even more.

"Congrats on getting the executive chef position," Sangeeta said.

"Thank you."

Sangeeta looked behind him. "Here's our bride. I'm hoping the groom will be able to make it as well."

A beautiful older woman approached, casually but tastefully dressed, and simply beaming.

"Hi, I'm Rajni." She offered her hand, and Karina and Aneel each shook it. "Thank you for doing this last minute."

"Of course," Karina said. "Happy to help, and it's a fabulous opportunity as well, from what I understand from Sangeeta."

"I hope so. Many of our friends have children who are engaged or getting engaged, so I certainly hope that all goes well, and they reach out to you." Rajni was warm and loving, and Aneel could tell that Karina liked her instantly.

Sangeeta moved them to a table. "The first thing I need to mention is that the camera crew from Fusion has reached out to me. They would like a bit of footage of Karina and the team catering this event as a follow-up to the competition they've been airing. They intend on doing more chef-related cooking competitions, so this footage would be sort of a 'where are they now' footage for use in the future. The fact that Aneel is here as well, will only add to the significance." She looked at

Rajni. "Very little of the wedding or reception will be filmed. It's meant to be a foodie type thing. How does everyone feel about this?"

They all looked at the bride.

"I'm fine. Anything to help young couples just starting out in their businesses." She smiled between Karina and Aneel.

"Oh. We're not together," Aneel said, not looking at Karina. "We just work together. I'm simply helping for this event."

Karina turned to him, a smile on her face, but her eyebrows furrowed for a quick second.

Rajni lingered her gaze on them for an extra second, her eyes narrowing. "Huh." She shook her head.

Karina opened her laptop. They both went through each item and how it would be made and served.

"We have some staff to help," Karina was saying, "but Aneel and I will be doing the cooking right here on-site."

"That's fabulous." Rajni was clearly pleased. She suddenly looked behind Aneel and broke out into a huge smile. "And here he is. My fiancé."

Footsteps sounded as the groom approached Aneel from behind and walked around him to Rajni. She raised her hands to him and pulled him close.

Aneel's heart stopped.

"Everyone, this is my fiancé, Yogesh Rawal." Rajni glowed.

Karina snapped her head to Aneel, but he hardly noticed. His father simply looked at him, speechless.

Aneel stood. "This is *your* wedding?" he growled at him.

Rajni looked from his dad to him, the confusion on her face turning to realization.

His father looked as surprised as he felt.

Sangeeta asked the question, "Do you know each other?"

Aneel barely heard her over the pounding in his head. This lavish, over-the-top event was to be his father's wedding.

His mother had barely been able to afford to go to the doctor.

"Yes," his father finally said. "This is my son."

Anger thundered in Aneel's chest as agitation crawled on his skin. His hand on the table shook with it, and Karina covered his hand with hers. She squeezed his hand, and he took comfort in it, pathetic soul that he was. This venue, this menu, the decor, the publicity, all of this was the makings of a dream wedding. A dream wedding for his father, who had done nothing but cause nightmares for his mother.

Everything, everything in his body and mind screamed for him to leave. Begged him not to do this. Get in the car, go home and refuse to cook for this wedding. Saira was right. It had been hard to grow up without a father. It had been hard to lose his mother too soon. It wasn't fair that his father got to live, and his mother did not.

Karina shifted in her seat, and her scent floated to him.

Everything in him told him not to cook for this wedding. Everything.

Except his heart.

He inhaled deeply and calmed himself with that citrus scent. Karina hadn't picked him. She had chosen another man. That in combination with the fact that this was his father's opulent wedding should have him running for his car in a rage.

It didn't matter. What mattered, what calmed him was the love he felt for the woman beside him. He could do this for her, with her. And he could do it happily.

He swallowed and opened his mouth to speak.

Before he could, Karina stood. "I'm sorry, Rajni. But Chef Rawal and I will not be able to cook for you this weekend."

Karina could hardly believe what she had just said, but she had meant it. The pain on Aneel's face was clear. It was also clear that he would do this. As much as it hurt him, he would do this for her. She couldn't let him.

Aneel stared at her with shock. Rajni and Sangeeta were speechless.

"I will reach out to Amar Virani and Divya Shah to cover. You will love them." She checked her phone. They likely were still in town; a simple call should do. She'd owe them for sure, but that was a problem for another day. They would also get the TV coverage. Win-win. She should have knots in her stomach, but she was strangely calm.

"What?" The bride finally found her voice and turned to Sangeeta.

The planner looked to Karina. "Chef Mistry. If there is a problem, I'll be more than happy to—"

"The problem is me," Aneel's father spoke.

Aneel put up a hand. "No. It's fine." His laugh was obviously forced. At least obvious to her. "Chef Mistry is a terrible jokester." He took her elbow, turning to the couple. "Give us a minute?" Without waiting for an answer, he gently steered her outside the hotel. He didn't stop walking until they were a few feet from the water.

"What are you doing?" he asked, still astonished. His eyes were wide with concern. "This is the opportunity of a lifetime for you."

"Not if it causes you this much pain." Karina stood firm. "I can't force you to do this."

"Karina. No one is forcing me. I meant what I said that day. I will always be there for you. Even…" he gestured behind them to the group waiting for them "…even now. I'm here. And I'm not going to leave."

"I can do this wedding alone." It would be crazy, but she'd find a way.

He grinned. "Of that, I have no doubt. But you don't have to. I will be there. I will cook by your side, like I promised. I realized something just this morning."

"What's that?"

"I always said that my mom wasn't happy, that she never got her happily-ever-after. But I was wrong, Karina." He paused. "Saira and I, we were her happily-ever-after. Saira has grown into this incredible woman." He tilted his head. "Questionable methods, every once in awhile, but her heart is in the right place." Tears lined his eyes. He swallowed. "And my mom gave me her gift of cooking, and I'm pretty good at it, I think."

Tears burned at her eyes as well. She took his hand. She was so proud of him.

"My father, sadly, missed out on all of that. He can never get that time back. He knows that. This..." he waved his hand all around at the wedding "...this is his chance at some level of happiness. I don't see the point in denying him." He gave her a side smile. "Especially when all this, is really about you and your future. And I'm here for you."

Karina's heart swelled as she simply took him in. *This man.*

"Aneel, I—"

"Chef Mistry." Sangeeta's voice came from behind her. "I'm sorry to interrupt, but I really need to know what's going on. There's a lot of money at stake—"

"It's fine, Sangeeta," Karina said, still smiling at the amazing man in front of her. "We'll do it."

Chapter Thirty-Five

Aneel arrived home in the early evening to find Tyler waiting for him outside his door. "Where's your key?"

"I didn't want to scare you."

Aneel shook his head as he opened the door.

"I've hardly seen you in a month," Tyler said as he followed Aneel in. "You've been busy with the competition and helping Karina with catering."

"It's called working."

"Helping Karina is not working."

"I get paid," Aneel countered, not sure why he had to make that distinction when the reality was that he would help Karina for free.

"Technicality and you know it." This was the problem with hanging out with people you have known since childhood. They knew you too well. Aneel recalled the way Karina had looked at him today, the way she had been willing to give up so much, just to save him some pain. His heart warmed.

"Whatever," Tyler was saying. "Let's go out. Drink and eat. Celebrate the new executive chef."

Aneel studied his friend. He was right. He hadn't been around for a while. "That sounds great. Mind if I take a shower?"

"Please do." Tyler plopped himself on the sofa and turned on the TV. "You get a pay raise?"

"And better benefits."

"Great. Let's find you a grown-up place to live in then," Tyler called.

Tyler was right. It was about time Aneel found a house or something. Paying rent for this place was not his long-term plan. Though to be honest, his long-term plan had likely included a wife and family. Images of Karina bombarded him. He pushed them aside for now. Aneel finished his shower and donned decent jeans and a long-sleeve T-shirt.

"I do need a real place," Aneel said as he came out to the family room. "Set me up with whoever helped Saira."

"That would be me." Tyler cleared his throat and looked away.

"Perfect. Then help me find a place." Aneel eyed his friend. "You going to tell me more about that 'gorgeous lawyer'?"

"No," Tyler said. "Tonight is all about you."

Aneel grunted as he grabbed his leather jacket on the way out. They walked a few blocks in the pleasant evening chill and stopped in at their favorite bar to have a beer.

"What's going on?" Tyler asked as he sipped his beer. "For a guy who has the dream job he wanted, you look...underwhelmed."

Aneel shrugged. The way Karina had looked at him today was promising, but he could not ignore the fact that Chirag was back.

"Karina or your dad?" Tyler asked.

"Both. Neither." Aneel gulped his beer.

"Your dad's getting married?"

Aneel nodded.

"That pisses you off."

"Not as much as you might think. That wedding I'm helping her with, it's my dad's." Aneel sipped his beer, the bitter taste welcome.

Tyler's blue eyes nearly bugged out of his head. "Bro."

"Yep."

"You must really love that woman," Tyler said as he raised his glass.

Aneel was unable hide to his grin. "I do, but that's beside the point."

Tyler chuckled. "It *is* the point."

"It doesn't matter." Aneel looked at his friend, his brother. "She wants to give her ex a chance. He's the father of her child. I can't stand in the way." He took another gulp of his beer, then stared into it. "You know what scares me?"

"What?"

"He's a good guy." And there it was. Chirag was not the complete jerk Aneel was hoping he would be. He was a good guy. He could make both Veer and Karina happy.

Tyler furrowed his brow. "Isn't that a good thing?"

"It's a great thing." Aneel sat up. "He seems to really be showing up for Veer."

Tyler placed a hand on Aneel's shoulder. "You're scared she won't pick you."

Chirag had made reservations at a nice place for them that night. Her father took Veer for "outside food" and Karina borrowed a dress from Sona's closet and changed while Chirag waited. She came down twenty minutes later to find Sona, Rani and Param waiting for her.

Rani held up her phone. "Group chat."

She looked around. "Where is he?"

Chirag raised a hand. "Over here."

Karina made a move, but the women just glared at her. Param raised his eyebrows at her and leaned toward her. "My brothers and sisters-in-law were itching to come over, too."

Karina grinned. Family was everything. She let them do their thing.

The two women sauntered up to him. "Expensive cologne," Sona said.

"Quality shirt and fashionable sweater." Rani shrugged.

"Let me see your hands," Sona ordered.

Chirag obliged.

"Nicely manicured." Rani studied him. "You're a lawyer." It was an accusation.

"Yes..." he answered.

Rani raised an eyebrow and glanced at Karina before looking at Chirag. "Veer's birthday," Rani demanded.

"July 16," Chirag answered without hesitation.

Karina snapped her head to him, as did every other person in the room.

"A good start, but we'll see," Rani said, narrowing her eyes at Chirag.

The three of them headed for the kitchen, and Karina smiled sweetly and they left, each one glaring at Chirag as they went.

She offered Chirag no apology for their behavior.

"Can't say I blame them. I'd be the same if I had a sister," Chirag said, but he looked relieved that they were gone all the same. "Shall we?"

"Of course." Karina led the way out of the house. Fall was definitely here, a chill in the air. She wrapped her shawl tightly around her.

He opened the passenger door of his car for her before he sat down in the driver's seat.

"What, no limo today?" She smirked.

His eyes widened. "Oh. I thought you'd like just driving. I can get the limo in a minute."

She chuckled. "I'm just kidding. This is perfect."

He drove, and they chatted. She told him about Veer as a baby, and he listened, absorbing everything she said about their son, asking questions about details that he had missed.

"If you have baby pictures you're willing to share, I'd love to see them," Chirag said.

Karina nodded. "We all have pictures. I can send you some."

They arrived at a fancy Italian restaurant, and Chirag had a valet park the car. He opened doors, pulled out her chair and did all the gentlemanly things. Once seated, he ordered a bottle of wine. "So, what about you?" he asked.

"What about me?" she asked, perusing the appetizers on the menu. A few caught her eye, and she wondered what Aneel would have thought about the fancy combinations.

"How have you been?"

She felt Chirag's intense attention upon her. She closed the menu and looked at him. Really looked at him. She had always found him handsome. He still was. He filled out his shirt and sweater well, no longer the lanky young man she had known. His eyes were the same dark brown as Veer's, but while they held longing, they didn't hold the gentleness of the brown eyes she'd recently come to favor. And just like that, her mind wandered to earlier that morning when Aneel had agreed to help her cater his father's wedding, regardless of how it affected him.

Her body warmed at the thought.

"Karina?"

She brought herself back to the moment. "I just try to get through each day without screwing up too much." She grinned at him.

Someone came to pour their wine. They clinked glasses and sipped, Chirag's eyes never leaving hers. "You know, I didn't just get income from working. I inherited a large amount from a distant relative."

"Seriously?" Karina gaped at him.

Chirag laughed and nodded. "It was a huge surprise to me, but there it is. I'd like to open an account for Veer—for his future." He touched her hand. "I'd also like to take care of you. An attempt at making up for when I wasn't there for you all these years. I'm willing to spend the rest of my life making that up to you."

Karina stared at him as the waiter dropped off warm bread. Chirag was serious. He loved her, and he was remorseful, and he wanted to take care of his son and her.

She studied him. His smile was genuine. And that was most certainly affection, or maybe love for her, in his eyes.

She searched her heart. She felt nothing. Nothing at all.

Not true. She held fondness for him. She was happy he'd turned his life around and was in a better place—but that was all. As handsome and charming as he was, there was no attraction. His hand was still on hers, but she hardly noticed. It was certainly nothing like the electric sensation she had when Aneel's pinkie so much as grazed hers at work.

She had been willing to give up the biggest catering job she had to keep Aneel from experiencing the pain of catering his father's wedding. Maybe that's how it was when you were in love. You made sacrifices, but they didn't feel like sacrifices because you were happy to do them.

Because that was it, wasn't it? She was in love. With Aneel.

Her heart thudded in rapid fire as if rejoicing in the fact that she had finally come to this realization.

"Say something," he said, but sadness already flickered in his eyes.

"Chirag, I—I believe you. Everything. I can see that you are a changed man. That you are interested in being part of Veer's life. And that brings me such joy, that you are here for him."

"But…"

"But—" she sagged "—I don't have those feelings for you. I don't know that I ever did. We weren't together that long, and then I was pregnant…" She held up her hands. "I'm sorry.

I want you in Veer's life. But not in mine. Not like that." She bent down to pick up her bag.

She needed to see Aneel. He was the one that made her heart pound. He was the one she was thinking about all the time. In the chaos of their morning meeting, she had left things unsaid. Things like how she loved bantering with him. How she loved when he challenged her.

How she loved *him*.

"It's the chef, isn't it?" Chirag said softly. "It's not that it's obvious, but it's hard to hide or deny that kind of bond."

"It is the chef," she confessed, sitting up. She felt lighter than she had in a long while.

"Don't go. Stay," Chirag insisted. His eyes looked glassy, but he looked at her and smiled. "If we're going to co-parent, we should get to know each other better, as we are now, don't you think?" He looked at her, a plea in his eyes.

"Chirag—"

He inhaled deeply into a sigh. "I knew it was a long shot, that you would love me. There's someone out there for me. I was hoping it was you, but clearly it's not." He met her eyes. "Please stay. We have this wonderful wine… Let's build a friendship, a real connection this time. For Veer."

She considered him for a moment. He kept surprising her. Of course she should get to know him. Karina picked up her wineglass. "Okay. What's good here?" She took a sip of her wine. It really was good.

"Well." Chirag's pleasure was clear. "I was hoping you would tell me. Let's do the tasting menu, and you critique."

"I love doing that." She laughed, finally relaxed.

Chapter Thirty-Six

Tyler insisted that they celebrate Aneel's promotion at a fancy restaurant on him. "You don't think we should hold off celebrating until my sister is available?" Aneel asked.

"She's meeting us for dinner," Tyler told him.

The Uber dropped them off at a gorgeous restaurant. "This is like a date-night restaurant, Tyler."

"Yeah, true. But the food is fabulous." Tyler walked ahead.

They entered to a crowd at the hostess station. Saira waved at them. Of course she had snagged a table. Aneel made his way toward his sister.

She stood as they approached and wrapped her brother in a huge hug. "Executive chef, huh? How will we fit that giant ego through the door?" She squeezed hard and whispered, "I'm so proud of you, Bhaiya."

He returned her hug and then pulled back to look at her. She was dressed for the occasion, dress pants, nice blouse and something was different about her hair. A couple tears fell from her eyes, and she expertly wiped them away without touching her makeup. She didn't look like that little girl he remembered or even the college girl who used to walk around barely showered in his hand-me-down sweats. A pang of love and nostalgia hit his chest as he realized that his sister was all grown up.

"I'm proud of you, too," he said.

She narrowed her eyes at him. "You feeling okay?"

He laughed. "I'm great."

They sat down, and Tyler ordered them a bottle of wine while they looked at the menu.

"Let's do the tasting menu and Bhaiya can critique," Saira said. "It *is* his favorite thing to do in a fancy restaurant."

"Sounds good to me," Aneel said. He let Tyler do all the ordering. They finished one bottle of wine. His mind of course drifted to Karina. He knew she was out with Chirag tonight. The thought put an ache in his heart. He pushed it away. Tonight was about new beginnings. Celebration.

Then, as if he'd conjured her with his thoughts, he saw her sitting at a small table for two, tucked away by a window. He could not tear away his gaze. Chirag's hand was on hers, and they were laughing.

Tyler stopped talking and followed his gaze. "Aw, crap." He paused. "Let's go."

Aneel shook his head. "No. That's fine. We already ordered. Saira's here. We're celebrating. It's a good day. It's fine. I'll be fine." He glanced at Karina again and felt Tyler and Saira share a look.

He was anything but fine. He had a clear view of their table and her. She had on a dark blue dress that showed off strong arms and legs. Huh. He'd never really seen her legs. Her hair was not in a messy bun or ponytail but instead flowed in dark waves down her back and shoulders. Just as he'd always imagined but never actually seen.

Aneel watched as Chirag paid the bill, and they stood. Chirag put his hand on her lower back, and Aneel's heart dropped like a stone into his stomach. A mild buzzing filled his ears as he zeroed in with superhuman sight to that hand on *her* back.

He could still feel his own hand at her back, protective and, if he was honest, *claiming*. He remembered clearly the feeling of her leaning into that touch, glancing at him with peace in her eyes, trusting him. She had felt grounded by his touch, safe.

As if she could feel his eyes on her, she turned toward him. He knew when she saw him because her eyes popped open in surprise, and she froze for just a second before her gaze dropped quickly to Chirag's hand on her back. She flicked her eyes to Aneel, and even from distance, he could see the apology on her face.

Saira also turned, and Karina raised her hand and smiled as she walked toward them.

Karina and Chirag were clearly on a date at the restaurant. Aneel had already known that was happening—he just hadn't thought he would be witness to it. None of this prevented Aneel from noticing how stunning she was in that dress. The navy blue fabric hugged her curves in a way that even her leggings couldn't. He'd always been drawn to Karina's natural beauty; the way she looked tonight was simply another iteration of a stunning woman.

She stopped in front of them and made eye contact with Tyler first. "Hey, Tyler. Good to see you."

"You, too," Tyler said.

She smiled at his sister. "Saira. Looking lovely."

"Um, thanks. Beautiful dress." Saira flicked her eyes toward Aneel.

Aneel used every bit of strength to put a smile on his face. Chirag was standing there, grinning, his full attention on Karina.

"Sunshine," Karina said. "Looks like a fabulous celebration. Well deserved."

He could only nod.

"Oh, uh. Chirag, this is Tyler and Saira." She nodded at them. "This is Veer's father, Chirag."

Handshakes and mumbled "nice to meet yous" all around, but Aneel could not take his eyes off Karina, a jealous rage burning inside him. No matter that this was what Karina wanted, he was surprised that he did not actually turn green.

Karina dressed up was the icing on the cake, a treat for all his senses. Her citrus scent was as delicious as ever. He'd never give up the messy buns and ponytails, except for the chance to free her hair and run his fingers—

"Aneel." Tyler nudged him with his knee.

"What?" Aneel was still taking in Karina.

"She's talking to you," Tyler murmured.

"Sorry. Maybe had an extra drink or two." Aneel's voice was sharp, and his words came out clipped.

Karina looked confused but rallied. "Sure, Sunshine, whatever. I was just asking if you ordered the tasting menu?" She ran her gaze over him. "You clean up nice."

"We did. It's Bhaiya's favorite thing to do," Saira said. "Deconstruct."

Karina gave a small smile at that. "It's a strong talent he has."

Aneel said nothing.

Silence floated, thick and unwelcome between them. Normally, Aneel would fill it with a joke or story. He simply gulped at his wine.

"Well. We should be going then." Karina smiled. "See you for prep tomorrow, Sunshine?"

Tyler and Saira said their goodbyes, and Aneel simply nodded. Just to torture himself a bit more, he watched her leave. A child needed their father. He of all people knew that. Knew it better than most, in fact. He couldn't compete with that. He *shouldn't* compete with that.

"You are done for." Tyler was shaking his head at him.

"That's her ex-husband?" Saira's eyes went wide.

"Yes."

"Bhaiya." She shook her head and turned to look at Tyler and Aneel. "That man is hot. Hot hot."

Tyler stared at her. "He's not that good-looking."

"Um. Yes. He is." She craned her neck to look again. "All angles."

"You're not helping." Tyler waved his hand toward Aneel.

"Bhaiya's handsome. I think?" She moved back as if to take a proper look at him.

Aneel rolled his eyes at her. "Make yourself useful and order another bottle."

Tyler clicked his tongue. "You are so completely head over heels in love with that woman, if she doesn't pick you, it's going to take me and your sister a long time to pick up the pieces."

Aneel turned back to his friend. "You can start by pouring the next bottle." He ran his gaze wistfully at the exit and caught Chirag opening the door for her. "Because she didn't pick me."

Karina stepped out of the restaurant into the chill of the evening, draping her shawl around herself. Her thoughts were on the small group still inside.

"Karina." Chirag's voice was sharp.

"What?" She looked at him.

He shook his head at her and smiled. "I've been trying to get your attention, but you seem a hundred miles away." He turned toward the restaurant. "Or maybe only a hundred or so feet."

She glanced toward the door. Veer was safe at home with her father and Sona. The man she loved was inside, thinking that she did not love him.

"Go," Chirag said as the valet brought his car around. He leaned over and kissed her cheek. "Go get the love you deserve."

"Chirag, I'm—"

"Don't you dare say you're sorry. I had my chance. I blew it. Don't make the same mistake I did." He glanced toward the restaurant.

Karina was almost giddy. She barely waited until Chirag got in his car before turning back and going back into the restaurant.

The second bottle had just been corked when that familiar citrus scent floated to him. He must really have it bad if he was smelling her everywhere now.

"Aneel." Her voice was soft and hesitant, and right in front of him. He looked up and there she was, still in that dress, smiling at him.

"Karina."

Just her name added an electricity that even the sommelier noticed. She stopped and drew her gaze over the group as if unsure what to do. Tyler nodded at the poor woman and she hastily put the bottle on the table and withdrew herself.

"Is everything okay?" His first thought was that Chirag was not the nice guy he thought he was and had somehow left Karina here. But she didn't look put out. She looked...happy.

"Everything is great," she said, nodding. But she didn't move. Didn't move her gaze from his. "I...um...well I wanted to toast you," she said, suddenly flustered. "I sent Chirag home. I hope you don't mind, I didn't mean to crash—"

"Actually. No. You're fine." Tyler stood and motioned for Saira to do the same. "Saira and I were just going to go to the bar."

Saira stood. "Yep. To the bar. For a drink."

All four of them ignored the full bottle of wine the sommelier had left behind.

Tyler took Saira's hand and they went...somewhere. Aneel did not bother to take notice. All he noticed was Karina. And she was still standing.

"Have a seat." Aneel motioned to the chair Saira had just vacated.

She sat down next to him.

"How was dinner?" he asked.

"You really want to talk about how my dinner was?" Karina asked.

He shrugged.

"Okay. Well, it was fine. If you define 'fine' as all I could do was think about you," Karina said softly.

Aneel froze.

"All I wanted was to find you and tell you..." She hesitated, a deep flush in her cheeks. "I don't know why I'm so nervous." She chuckled and sniffled and he saw tears in her eyes. "I love you. I am not sure when I fell for you. But just now, sitting with Chirag, all I wanted was to come find you and tell you that I love you."

Aneel stared at her for a moment, unbelieving the words she had said.

"Aneel?" she asked.

He lifted his hand and tucked back a stray piece of hair. He let his fingers graze the silken skin of her jaw and cupped her face. He was certain she could hear the thud of his heart trying to get to her. He leaned toward her until their breath mingled between them. "I love you more than Veer loves the Avengers."

She started to smile, but he closed the small gap between them, placing his mouth on hers, finally finding home, and kissed her. She melted into him, and Aneel did not care that they were in a restaurant, that his sister was feet away. His only thought was that this was Karina who he loved, and she had picked him.

Chapter Thirty-Seven

The wedding was a huge success. Karina thoroughly enjoyed having Aneel by her side as they quite successfully executed the food for this wedding. While Aneel may not have made peace with his father, he was certainly not about denying him his wedding anymore.

It did take quite a bit of her self-control not to kiss him every chance she got, but they certainly made up for it when they were home alone.

They packed up the vans and Aneel had followed her home to help her unload. They left all the things in the mudroom to be dealt with in the morning.

Aneel drew her to him, his hands at her waist. "You were spectacular tonight," he said.

"Show me," she said.

He sighed deep. "If you insist." He leaned down and placed his mouth on hers and she leaned into him like a starved animal. She had told him she wasn't ready for "sleepovers" yet, and in this moment, she could not remember why. Maybe they didn't have to actually *sleep over*…

When they parted, out of breath and dazed, he produced a small jar from his pocket.

The cloves. From Uganda. It had been so long since they discussed this, she had thought maybe he forgot.

Karina's eyes widened. "They came in?"

Aneel nodded. "They came in a couple days ago, but we were busy with the wedding."

Still leaning on him, she took the jar from him and stared at it for a few moments. Inside could be the connection to her mother she had been searching for. Or it could just be cloves. She may never find the proper ingredients for the exact same masala her mother had made. Did that mean she wasn't connected to her?

When she had given birth, she had truly missed her mother. But then Rani had held her hand in the delivery room. Sona had helped with night feedings. Her father had helped with bathing a newborn. Did she miss her mother?

Yes.

Did that mean she wasn't connected to her? No. Connections to her mother were all around her, not only in this chai masala. Veer's laugh echoed in her head. So much like her mom's.

"You okay?" Aneel asked. "We don't have to—"

"No." She looked up at him. "I want to give it a try. It's just..." She looked down at the jar.

Aneel waited for her to look up at him again.

"It's just, it's okay. It's okay if these cloves don't work. I'm still connected to my mom through my sisters, my dad, even Veer. It's not just the masala."

She entered the kitchen and opened the jar. She inhaled the spicy aroma of the cloves before tossing them in a pan for a quick roast.

Aneel pulled out the other ingredients and the grinder. Without needing to speak, they roasted and ground the spices into a final mixture.

Karina met Aneel's eyes as she dipped her pinky into the dry masala. She couldn't put it to her tongue. "I can't taste it," she told him.

He put her pinky in his mouth and tasted. She studied his

expressionless face. "Let's make one cup of chai and taste it that way," he suggested.

She nodded. "You do it."

Aneel simmered the water, added the loose tea and their latest masala mix. He strained it into a mug for her and waited.

Karina's stomach was in knots, her heart pounding as she wrapped her hands around the warm mug, inhaled. The aroma was wonderful. But then she had always found comfort in the aroma of fresh chai. She had been denying herself this comfort for years.

No more.

She sipped. She looked up from her chai and found Aneel watching her. "It's delicious." Tears burned at her eyes.

He nodded. "But…"

"But it's not it."

He stepped in closer to her, gently took her mug and set it down, before wrapping her in his embrace. She closed her eyes and melted into his chest. He smelled of all the spices they had just used. Sweet cinnamon and cardamom, spicy clove, sharp black pepper and tangy nutmeg.

It really was okay. She pulled back to look at him. "You know. Fifteen years is a long time to try to replicate something."

"We can keep trying."

"No." Karina shook her head. "Let's just make our own." She inhaled the scent of him again. "And we'll make new memories to go with it."

Five months later

Karina sipped her steaming hot chai on the sofa, Veer curled up next to her, watching *Blue's Clues* while he defrosted. The cardamom was stronger in this batch of masala she and Aneel had made, the flavor reminding her of the gulab jamun they had made together at his apartment months ago.

She checked her email, noting a few new requests for catering. Maybe Chirag could help her get a website going. Sona had been taking photos of her events these past few months that might be useful for that.

"Mom?"

"Hmm."

"Why do you think Hulk is the best?" Veer sat up. His hair was tousled in his face, he needed a haircut.

Karina closed her laptop and stood. Veer jumped off the sofa and took her hand. "I might change my mind on that."

"So you agree it's Captain America?" Veer asked as they went upstairs.

"I'm thinking Captain Marvel."

Veer sighed deeply as if he could not believe her answers. Karina grinned. She loved these slower mornings that allowed her to talk to her son and get him ready for school. Her dad and Sona had already left for the day.

"Remember, you dad is going to pick you up today and you're sleeping over there. I have a late event tonight." Veer would have been fine here with her dad, but Chirag enjoyed having Veer over and visa-versa.

Veer grinned up at her, a bit of mischief in his eyes as he actually rolled them at her. That was a first. "I know. I know."

"Okay," Karina said.

He dressed and she quickly gave him breakfast before dropping him off to school. She was catering a small engagement party tonight, so her first stop was the farmers market. No more than twenty people, she had been told. She started, as always, with the produce.

"Hey." A familiar voice grumbled at her ear, kissing her neck. She leaned into Aneel and turned to face him.

"Well, good morning to you too." She wrapped her arms around his neck and took him in. The smile, the desire in his eyes. She touched the edge of his hair, he needed a haircut too.

"Menu all set for your event tonight?"

"Yes. Should be done by ten. Veer is sleeping over at Chirag's…" She pursed her lips at him.

Aneel furrowed his brow in confusion. "What will you do all night?"

"I'll think of something." She leaned up and kissed him.

"We should finish our shopping." Aneel groaned as he pulled back from the kiss. "We're blocking the produce."

Karina finished cooking just in time for the 5pm delivery. She freshened up and changed into her good whites for the delivery. She wasn't familiar with the address, but this was a new client. She found the place easily, as it wasn't far from her father's house. Beautiful townhome in a gorgeous suburban neighborhood, just past Veer's school. She grabbed a few things and walked up to the front door and rang the bell.

She thought about meeting Aneel later that night…

The door opened and she nearly dropped the food. Standing in front of her, wearing dress pants and a light blue button down shirt, sporting a new haircut and looking at her with that side smile and dimples was Aneel.

What was he doing here? He needed to be at Fusion. Was he catering now? Why was he dressed up?

She opened her mouth but nothing came out.

Aneel reached over and took the food from her. "Come in."

She stared at him and numbly nodded. "What…? Why aren't you at work? Why are you *here*?"

Aneel put the food down and closed the door. "I bought this house."

"You bought a house?" She looked around with new eyes. The inside was also beautiful, if not very empty.

"I bought a house," he confirmed.

"It's empty."

He nodded. "Yeah…about that." He paused. "Come." She

followed him as he walked to the kitchen. His scent wafted to her and drew her toward him. She would never tire of it, that soap and leather scent.

She froze as Aneel stepped aside with a small flourish and presented the kitchen. The house did not look like it would have a kitchen this size, but it was the same size as the one in her father's house, if not bigger.

"This kitchen is incredible. The appliances. The counter space. And that fridge—"

"There's another one in the garage," Aneel said. "Just through the mudroom door."

Her eyes bugged open. "I... Wow!" She was speechless.

He sighed, seeming to relax. "I was hoping you would say that." He motioned to the barstools at the island. "Please, sit down."

She eyed him as she took a seat. He sat down next to her. He was fidgety. He swallowed. "Karina. I—"

"Yes." She nodded at him with great enthusiasm.

"Yes, what? I didn't ask you anything." He smirked at her.

"You're going to ask me to marry you." Her smile must take up her whole face, but she couldn't control it. It was as if all her happiness was leaking out of her in that smile.

"How do you know that?"

She looked at him. He was cute. She put up one finger. "You bought a house with a huge kitchen that is located near Veer's school." She put up a second finger. "You're all dressed up." A third finger. "You got a haircut." Fourth, fifth and then all ten fingers went up. "And I love you more than anything and I've never been happier and the only reason you would do all this was if you wanted to marry me. And I do want to marry you, very much."

"Do you want the ring?" Aneel raised an eyebrow as he nodded and broke into a smile that continued to grow across his face.

"There's a ring?" She melted.

"There's always a ring."

"But there's a kitchen—" she started. But then Aneel presented her with the most beautiful solitaire, round cut diamond ring. She gasped. "There's a ring."

He placed it on her finger.

"There's deep declarations of love and commitment, too," he said as he leaned toward her, cupping her head in his hands, his mouth finding hers.

She leaned into him, kissing him back, taking all those declarations of love and commitment. "I don't need all this. I just need you."

"I'm yours." He went back to kissing her just as the mudroom door banged open.

"Can we come in?" Veer's voice reached her. "Is the surprise over?"

Aneel looked over his shoulder at Veer. "Yes, it is."

Veer raised his eyebrows at Aneel in expectation. "What did she say?"

Karina looked at Aneel, then at her son, aware that her family had already known and was slowly filtering in.

Aneel left her side and knelt down next to Veer. "You were right, buddy. She said yes."

* * * * *

Look for Saira's story,
the next installment in Mona Shroff's
miniseries Once Upon a Wedding.
Coming soon to Harlequin Special Edition!